At Issue

I The Affordable Care Act

Other Books in the At Issue Series:

At Issue

I The Affordable Care Act

Tamara Thompson, Book Editor

GREENHAVEN PRESS
A part of Gale, Cengage Learning

Farmington Hills, Mich • San Francisco • New York • Waterville, Maine
Meriden, Conn • Mason, Ohio • Chicago

GALE
CENGAGE Learning

Elizabeth Des Chenes, *Director, Content Strategy*
Douglas Dentino, *Manager, New Product*

© 2015 Greenhaven Press, a part of Gale, Cengage Learning.

WCN: 01-100-101

LIBRARY OF CONGRESS CATALOGING-IN-PUBLICATION DATA

The Affordable Care Act / Tamara Thompson, Book Editor.
     pages cm. -- (At issue)
 Includes bibliographical references and index.
 ISBN 978-0-7377-7149-7 (hardcover) -- ISBN 978-0-7377-7150-3 (pbk.)
 1. United States. Patient Protection and Affordable Care Act. 2. Health insurance--Law and legislation--United States. 3. Health care reform--United States. I. Thompson, Tamara, editor.
   KF3605.A328201A2 2014a
   346.73'086382--dc23
                                                                2014021942

Printed in the United States of America
1 2 3 4 5 6 7 18 17 16 15 14

Contents

Introduction

President Barack Obama's watershed health-care law, the Patient Protection and Affordable Care Act, is the biggest regulatory overhaul of the American health-care system since Congress approved the Medicare and Medicaid health insurance programs in 1965. It is also one of the most hotly contested, publicly maligned, and politically divisive pieces of legislation the country has ever seen.

Popularly known as the Affordable Care Act (ACA), or simply "Obamacare," the complex and far-reaching health-care reform bill has barely survived numerous near-death experiences after being signed into law March 23, 2010. Since its passage, the ACA has endured a Supreme Court challenge to its constitutionality; repeated congressional efforts to repeal, defund, or postpone its provisions; a government shutdown intended to block its enactment; lawsuits by twenty-eight states trying to avoid participation; additional lawsuits challenging the payment of federal tax subsidies to consumers who buy insurance through the program; daunting implementation challenges; a disastrous launch of its online insurance marketplace and enrollment system; and widespread public disenchantment because the program did not unfold the way the president promised it would.

Despite such formidable challenges, the main provisions of the ACA were enacted January 1, 2014, on schedule. Additional elements of the program will continue to roll out through 2020, although various deadlines and requirements have been adjusted and details will continue to be modified as events unfold throughout the multiyear process. Totaling more than two thousand pages, the Affordable Care Act is a complicated and sometimes confusing bundle of legislation, but the program itself is built around two simple goals: giving more

Americans better access to affordable, quality health insurance and reducing the growth of health-care spending in the United States.

The ACA increases access to affordable care in several ways, including a massive expansion of Medicaid with eased eligibility requirements so that millions of people can newly qualify for the government's free health insurance program for low-income families and individuals. The ACA also created health insurance exchanges, or "marketplaces," where folks who have higher earnings can purchase health-care policies from private companies. Available plans are divided into four tiers that vary according to price and cost-sharing percentages. Consumers who meet certain income requirements can have their monthly premium subsidized by government tax credits through the exchanges. Residents in thirty-six states can buy ACA-backed health-care policies online at Healthcare.gov, the insurance marketplace operated by the federal government, while fourteen states run their own ACA exchanges.

Since most people get health insurance through employers, the exchanges primarily serve individuals who buy their own coverage, but an "employer mandate" in the act requires employers with fifty or more full-time workers to offer insurance that meets ACA standards by January 2016 or face a penalty. Although businesses with fewer employees are not required to participate, a small-business insurance exchange is slated to open in November 2014. Starting in 2017, exchanges will have the option to include employers with more than one hundred employees.

Many of the key reforms in the ACA affect all health-care consumers and the insurance industry as a whole. To improve the quality of care and reduce the growth of spending, the ACA established landmark benefits, rights, and protections for consumers, as well as new regulations, goals, and incentives for insurance companies. Among the law's most popular provisions, insurers can no longer refuse coverage or charge higher premiums based on preexisting conditions or gender; young adults may now stay on a parent's insurance plan until age twenty-six; insurance companies can no longer increase premiums or drop subscribers when they get sick; and lifetime and annual coverage limits have been abolished.

Another big change is that all health-care policies must now include a minimum standard of "Ten Essential Benefits": outpatient care and chronic disease treatment, emergency services, hospitalization, maternity and newborn care, mental health services and addiction treatment, prescription drugs, rehabilitative services and devices, laboratory services, pediatric services, and free preventive and wellness services. Individually purchased insurance plans had to comply with these standards by January 1, 2014, a requirement that prompted a massive wave of policy cancellations nationwide. Some 4.7 million people received notices that their existing policies were being terminated because they didn't meet the new standards, contradicting President Obama's infamous and often repeated remark that, "if you like your plan, you can keep your plan" under the Affordable Care Act.

The American public was stunned and disillusioned by this turn of events, even more so when many replacement plans arrived with significantly higher premiums than the cancelled ones. Media coverage of the issue was scathing. A second wave of cancellations is expected after employer-sponsored policies become subject to the same essential benefits requirements in 2016. The American Enterprise Institute, a conservative think tank, predicts that as many as one hundred million noncompliant employer-sponsored policies could be terminated at that time, though as in the individual market, most of them will likely be modified and reoffered, though perhaps at a higher cost.

But policy cancellations aren't the only controversy surrounding the Affordable Care Act. Another major point of contention is the so-called individual mandate that requires all Americans to have health insurance—either from an employer, purchased privately, or through a government program—or pay a tax penalty (1 percent of income in 2014, 2 percent in 2015, and 2.5 percent in 2016). The penalty will be postponed two years for people whose existing policies were cancelled.

The individual mandate's legality was challenged in court, based on the argument that it constituted unpermitted government interference with free-market commerce. The US Supreme Court, however, upheld the mandate's constitutionality on June 28, 2012, ruling that the penalty falls under the purview of Congress's taxing authority. The individual mandate penalty is one of several taxes and fees designed to raise hundreds of billions of dollars over the next decade to help underwrite ACA reforms, including the Medicaid expansion and the government-subsidized plans bought on the exchanges. The tax-generating mechanisms of the act have drawn intense and ongoing criticism from Republicans, with conservative political commentator Rush Limbaugh characterizing the ACA as being a Trojan horse for "the biggest tax increase in the history of the world." Another controversial aspect of the act is the reason that there is an individual mandate in the first place.

The success of the Affordable Care Act is predicated on the model of a shared-risk pool—the idea that including young, healthy people in the program is essential to offset the likely higher expenses incurred by those who are older or sick. Mandating participation across the board makes it possible to offer everyone the same comprehensive services and to charge everyone the same premiums. In that way, the risks are shared, but so are the benefits. Some critics, however, maintain that the shared-risk model makes the ACA a form of socialized medicine, and they vehemently seek its repeal for that, if for no other reason.

Indeed, congressional Republicans have forced a vote to repeal, gut, change, defund, or postpone ACA provisions more than fifty times as of this writing, and their efforts have most certainly continued since. Conservatives persist in characterizing the Affordable Care Act as a government takeover of health care that is a slippery slope toward fully socialized medicine in the United States. They maintain that the individual mandate will destroy freedom and increase health-care costs, and they remain dedicated to repealing, defunding, or dismantling the act entirely.

Contrast that mindset with the following statement by the Senate Democratic majority leader, Harry Reid, and it becomes clear just how politically divisive this health-care reform legislation has become: "Passing the Affordable Care Act was the greatest single step in generations towards ensuring access to affordable, quality health care for every person in America, regardless of where they live or how much money they make." It remains to be seen whether the Affordable Care Act is the best cure for the ailing American health-care system, as Democrats maintain, or whether it heralds an era of burdensome taxation and government intrusion, as Republicans insist. History will ultimately be the judge of whether the health-care reforms brought about by the Affordable Care Act represent President Obama's most important domestic policy achievement or his biggest bureaucratic misstep.

The authors in *At Issue: The Affordable Care Act* represent a wide range of viewpoints concerning the potential benefits and consequences of the country's new health-care law.

1

ObamaCare: The Plan Is to Transition to "Single-Payer" Socialized Medicine

William F. Jasper

William F. Jasper is senior editor of The New American, *a bi-weekly news magazine published by the John Birch Society, a conservative political advocacy group.*

Politicians on both sides of the political spectrum agree that the Affordable Care Act (ACA) has been a disaster, but Republicans and Democrats have very different ideas about what the problem actually is. While Republicans object to the law as a government takeover of the health-care system and want the whole initiative scrapped, Democrats, on the other hand, are saying that the law is not living up to its potential because it does not go far enough toward establishing a single-payer system in the United States. Many prominent Democrats acknowledge that they envision a "single-payer" or "public option" system of health care, but these are simply code words for socialized medicine. The ACA is simply a wealth redistribution scheme, and it is clear that fully socialized medicine has been the liberals' ultimate goal for the program since the beginning.

It may be one of the very few things that Republicans and Democrats, liberals and conservatives, Left and Right can agree on: ObamaCare has been an embarrassing series of rolling disasters since it stumbled out of the starting gate on October 1. From the non-functional Healthcare.gov website fiasco to the cancellation of millions (soon to be tens of millions) of existing health insurance policies to the heartstopping sticker shock on replacement policies, the Patient Protection and Affordable Care Act (ACA) has drawn brickbats from critics all across the political spectrum.

However, while disapproval of ObamaCare is very widespread, the critic camps are poles apart concerning what should be done. According to Senate Majority Leader Harry Reid (D-Nev.), House Minority Leader Nancy Pelosi (D-Calif.), the Democratic Socialists of America, the Congressional Progressive Caucus, and other leading lights of the far Left, the real problem with ObamaCare is that it does not go far enough; the "solution," they say, is to go all the way to socialized medicine. But they don't have the conviction and courage to be that honest, so they say we must resurrect the "single payer/public option" alternative that was defeated during the 2009–2010 battle over ObamaCare in Congress. For millions of Americans, the terms "single payer" and "public option" do not carry the same negative connotations as "socialized medicine," which, of course, is why they were adopted as code words.

This past August [2013], Sen. Harry Reid told the Las Vegas PBS [Public Broadcasting Service] program, *Nevada Week in Review*, that ObamaCare is merely "a step" toward nationalized, government-run healthcare. The *Las Vegas Sun* report on the program carried this headline: "Reid says Obamacare just a step toward eventual single-payer system."

"Reid said he thinks the country has to 'work our way past' insurance-based health care," the *Sun* reported. "What we've done with Obamacare," Reid said, "is have a step in the right direction, but we're far from having something that's going to work forever."

When then asked by the PBS interviewer whether he meant ultimately the country would have to have a healthcare system that abandoned insurance as the means of accessing it, Reid replied: "Yes, yes. Absolutely, yes."

"We had a real good run at the public option—don't think we didn't have a tremendous number of people who wanted a single-payer system," Reid said, referring to the contentious battles over ObamaCare.

But political realities forced Reid to compromise; he had to settle for something less than fully socialized medicine. "We had to get a majority of votes," Reid told the PBS progam. "In fact, we had to get a little extra in the Senate, we have to get 60."

Reid knew that President Obama was blatantly lying when he repeatedly promised that under ObamaCare everyone who wanted to would be able to keep his current policy. Reid, Pelosi, Obama, and other architects of the ACA knew the sweeping law and its subsequent massive regulations (which are still being written) would cause upwards of 70 percent of individual policyholders to have their policies cancelled almost immediately. Tens of millions more would begin losing their coverage as various restrictions targeting employer-sponsored insurance (ESI) kicked in.

President Obama is publicly on the record for many years ... as an avid supporter of single-payer, socialized medicine, and despite his protestations to the contrary, is heading us precisely in that direction now.

This would drive millions of desperate Americans to look to the federal government to save them (from the destruction caused by the federal government's ACA), and that would be a good thing, the Reid-Pelosi-Obama cabal reasoned. But President Obama publicly insisted that ObamaCare critics were "not telling the truth" with claims he was trying to establish government-run healthcare.

Obama: No "Trojan Horse" for Socialized Medicine

In his June 15, 2009 address to the Annual Conference of the American Medical Association, President Obama declared that the ACA is not "a Trojan Horse for a single-payer system." He said:

> Let me also say that—let me also address a illegitimate concern that's being put forward by those who are claiming that a public option is somehow a Trojan horse for a single-payer system. I'll be honest; there are countries where a single-payer system works pretty well. But I believe—and I've taken some flak from members of my own party for this belief—that it's important for our reform efforts to build on our traditions here in the United States. So when you hear the naysayers claim that I'm trying to bring about government-run health care, know this: They're not telling the truth.

As we have reported before—and will recapitulate again, momentarily—President Obama is publicly on the record for many years (going back to his time as an Illinois State Senator and then as U.S. Senator) as an avid supporter of single-payer, socialized medicine, and despite his protestations to the contrary, is heading us precisely in that direction now.

Like Sen. Reid, Rep. Pelosi has made no secret of the fact that she has always wanted, and still wants, "single payer" nationalized, socialized healthcare. In a June 28, 2012 interview with Ed Schultz on MSNBC she explains that even though some on the far Left criticized ObamaCare for failing to enact single payer, it was a victory nonetheless, and would move us closer toward that goal:

SCHULTZ: Finally, is this Kennedy-like? You didn't get everything, but you got a great start. And you got some great things, and—that was kind of his philosophy. Take what you can get and move it forward?

NANCY PELOSI: Oh, well, we got much more than that. We got much more than that. Yes, Teddy [Kennedy] was the person who said, 'you have to—you have to see a victory and recognize it when it is in sight.' I wanted to have a bill that accomplished the same things as a single-payer or a public option would do. Even if we couldn't get the votes in the Senate to do the public option. And I believe we did that. I think we would have saved more money if we had the public option and I think that—but I think that our purposes are served by this. And if it enabled us to go forward, then so be it. One of these days, I still believe that we can—the decision, the judgment will be made, maybe by states about their doing single-payer on their own and the rest. But in the meantime, as far as meeting the needs of individuals and families there, and as I keep saying, as far as our families are concerned, the best is yet to come.

The best is yet to come? Sixteen months later, with the rollout of ObamaCare, millions of Americans now dispossessed of their healthcare would take umbrage at Pelosi's cheery prediction. This is the same Nancy Pelosi who infamously remarked on March 9, 2010, regarding the Affordable Care Act, "We have to pass the bill so that you can find out what is in it, away from the fog of controversy."

But one month into ObamaCare, with the fog of controversy thickening, Pelosi continued to declare her unalloyed praise for the ACA—and her continued commitment to a "public option" plan.

ObamaCare "was a heavy lift to pass," Pelosi told reporters on October 30. "I myself would've preferred single payer or public option, but this was a compromise, this is a compromise," she said. "But it does many of the things that we would've done under a public option. . . . I'm thrilled about the overarching plan. This is life, a healthier life, liberty to pursue your happiness, as our founders promised. Glitches will be worked out, and again, there's a lot of education that has to be done on something that is new."

Rep. Pelosi did not provide any citations from the founders of our constitutional republic to support the absurd proposition that they would have endorsed the federal government setting up a massive healthcare system and ordering citizens to purchase healthcare policies designed and dictated by federal bureaucrats. However, there are plenty of Marxist authorities whom she could cite and with whom she is undoubtedly familiar. Rep. Pelosi has been endorsed by the Democratic Socialists of America (DSA), one of the most influential Marxist groups in the country, and has spoken at DSA-sponsored events. She is a close ally of and promoter of the Congressional Progressive Caucus (CPC), the DSA-affiliated group of 80 of the most radical Democrats in the House of Representatives. The DSA and the CPC are some of the most persistent and influential promoters of single-payer socialized medicine.

On September 30, 2013, the eve of the ObamaCare rollout, the DSA web site featured a full-throated call by Gerald Friedman, a professor of economics at the University of Massachusetts at Amherst, to take ObamaCare all the way to full-blown government takeover. Friedman, a longtime labor activist and DSA member, argued:

> By eliminating perverse incentives for adverse selection, a single-payer plan would dramatically lower administrative costs and monopolistic pricing, saving nearly $600 billion, $5000 billion over a decade, while providing meaningful universal access.

> Barack Obama knows this and has been a long-time supporter of single payer. But as president, he accepted the long-standing political wisdom that it would be impossible to enact a single-payer program.

Friedman acknowledges that ObamaCare is a huge wealth redistribution scheme, which undoubtedly warms the cockles of his socialist heart. He writes: "Because the subsidies to help the newly insured buy coverage are paid largely through new taxes on the highest earners, the subsidized insurance will be one of the largest redistributive measures ever enacted."

Obama still intends to get to single-payer [health care], he simply understood that getting there by the direct route wasn't feasible.

But that isn't enough for the stalwart Marxists at DSA. Friedman continues:

After a century of struggle, the ACA commits the United States to providing universal access to health care. This is a great achievement, one to be treasured and nurtured. Now the real fight begins, to turn this commitment into a reality that the ACA itself cannot produce. Barack Obama was right the first time: only a single-payer program can provide universal coverage, and only a single-payer program can control costs. The ACA may be the last bad idea that Americans try, after it fails, we will finally do the right thing: single-payer health insurance.

That is what Friedman's socialist colleagues, such as Dr. Quentin Young and Dr. Steffi Woolhandler at the Physicians for a National Health Program (PNHP) are also pushing. The 90-year-old Dr. Young was active in the Communist Party back in the 1940s and has been active in many Communist Party fronts since then, as well as a longtime member of the Democratic Socialists of America. Dr. Young was one of the Chicago movers and shakers who met at the Hyde Park home of Weather Underground terrorists Bill Ayers and Bernadine Dohrn to launch the political career of Barack Obama. Politico.com interviewed Young in 2008 and reported:

"I can remember being one of a small group of people who came to Bill Ayers' house to learn that Alice Palmer was stepping down from the senate and running for Congress," said Dr. Quentin Young, a prominent Chicago physician and advocate for single-payer health care, of the informal gathering at the home of Ayers and his wife, Dohrn. "[Palmer] identified [Obama] as her successor."

Obama and Palmer "were both there," he said.

Drs. Young and Woolhandler have been harshly critical of ObamaCare because it did not go all the way to full socialized medicine. In an October 17, 2013 interview with Phil Kadner of Chicago's *Southtown Star*, Young noted that he has known Obama since before he was a senator. "Back then, he favored single-payer health care," Young said. "I don't know what happened, but something changed his mind."

Dr. Young has it wrong; Barack Obama has not changed his mind, he just changed his tactics. Obama still intends to get to single-payer, he simply understood that getting there by the direct route wasn't feasible; he would have to adopt a more deceptive, confusing, gradual, round-about route.

Drs. Young and Woolhandler, the DSA, CPC, and many others are now out there beating the drums for single-payer, pointing to the hopeless complexity and the notorious failures of ObamaCare. At some point, Obama, Pelosi, Reid, and other ACA champions will flip-flop and join them in calling for a transition from ObamaCare to single-payer socialized medicine. That has been their plan all along.

2

The Affordable Care Act Is Not Socialized Medicine

Victor Peña

Victor Peña is a director of health-care corporate initiatives with the American Cancer Society and a member of the American College of Healthcare Executives and National Forum for Latino Healthcare Executives.

A lot of people mistakenly believe that the Affordable Care Act (ACA) is socialized medicine. It is not, and it cannot be, because of a few simple facts about how the law works. First, health-care services under the act are provided by private physicians, hospitals, and insurance plans, not government-owned and -operated entities, as they would be under a socialized system. Second, the availability and pricing of plans is based on competition in the private sector marketplace, rather than by government price-setting. Third, the ACA does not dictate what kind of treatment an individual will receive; it simply sets minimum standards for essential services that must be made available. Calling the ACA socialized medicine is simply a distraction from the real issue at hand—the urgent need for significant health-care reform.

Many Americans have an inherent aversion to socialism or anything that remotely resembles a socialist political idea. They argue that the United States is and should be committed to free markets.

Victor Peña, MBA, "Decoding Health Care: Why 'Obamacare' Is Not Socialized Medicine," *Boyle Heights Beat*, September 27, 2013. Copyright © 2013 by Victor Peña. All rights reserved. Reproduced by permission.

In a socialist nation, the government controls all means of production and distribution of goods—and this often limits innovation and entrepreneurship.

Because the Affordable Care Act—Obamacare—promises to provide access to health care to millions of uninsured Americans and also requires citizens to purchase health insurance, some people believe that it is "socialized medicine." This could not be further from the truth. Those who believe that Obamacare is socialized medicine do not truly understand what socialized medicine is and base their assumptions on false information.

The term socialized medicine took hold during the cold war; it was meant to brand anyone advocating for universal access to health care as a communist. This phrase continues to be bandied about as the Affordable Care Act approaches a critical point in its implementation this October [2013].

The reality is that Obamacare is not socialized medicine, as many opponents of this law like to argue. There are major flaws in their argument—and it is important to note that most national healthcare systems in the world are not "socialized."

Developed nations that have universal health care systems often offer high quality services at a reasonable cost using private physicians, private hospitals and private insurance plans. In essence, in most other countries with universal access, the health care providers compete for business. These are not features of a "socialist" health care system.

Plenty of Competition

Obamacare aims to lower the costs of providing care in our health care system, while offering high quality services through the private sector. In California alone, more than ten insurance plans will be competing for your business under our state exchange—Covered California. Covered California is the online marketplace where California residents can purchase an affordable health insurance plan beginning October 1.

In practice, many Americans rather government run health insurance systems. Our Medicare system covers about 50 million Americans—one out of six. In this system, the government sets the rules, collects the premiums and pays the bills, though it does not employ providers. (Medi-Cal in California) is also a government-run health insurance system that provides 58 million Americans with access to care.

Under Obamacare, the federal government cannot dictate what kind of treatment or care you will obtain at any health care organization. That is left up to you.

Although Medicare and Medicaid are not always efficient, millions of Americans benefit. They are among the most important health care resources for residents of communities throughout Los Angeles County, including Boyle Heights.

Many opponents of the Affordable Care Act argue that they do not want to be forced to purchase a health plan and worry that the government will dictate the kind of care that they will receive or not receive. These claims are completely false and uninformed.

Under Obamacare, the federal government cannot dictate what kind of treatment or care you will obtain at any health care organization. That is left up to you and your health care provider. Many states will be regulating their respective health-care systems and resources, but no one should be denied care and the government will not pick and choose how you are treated when you are sick.

October 2013 will bring a new era for millions of Americans who lack health care access due to cost or pre-existing conditions, such as diabetes or heart disease. Millions of low-income California residents will now have the opportunity to access affordable health plans, including Medi-Cal, through Covered California.

Cost Savings Likely

Our health care system is highly inefficient and hugely expensive. We now have an opportunity to curb some of these growing costs in order to save our health care system in the long-term. The cost of insurance may become lower over time as more people purchase insurance, spreading the risk over a large pool of people. In fact, it is very important that the younger and healthier segment of our communities sign up for insurance coverage because including them will help lower the costs of insurance over time.

The bottom line is that the Affordable Care Act is not as "socialized" as many opponents want you to believe. We should scrutinize the risk of not doing anything about fixing our health care system instead of arguing whether or not Obamacare is a socialist plan.

3

The Affordable Care Act Falls Short of Health Care as a Human Right

Anja Rudiger

Anja Rudiger is director of programs at the National Economic and Social Rights Initiative (NESRI), a nonprofit that works with communities to build a broad movement for economic and social rights, including health, housing, education, and work with dignity.

Although opponents of the Affordable Care Act (ACA) have said the program is a Trojan horse that represents the first step toward a publically funded, single-payer health-care system, such an outcome is not likely to develop from such a fundamentally flawed program. In reality, the ACA is little more than a stopgap attempt to rein in health-care spending, and the program is riddled with serious inequalities, both economic and racial. Most glaringly, the ACA will leave millions of the very poorest uninsured because the Supreme Court allowed states to opt out of expanding their Medicaid programs as part of the ACA. The ACA falls far short of universal coverage, so it is time to look past this inadequate model and push for truly universal and equitable health care for all and for the recognition of health care as a basic human right.

The intense media hype around the troubled Obamacare roll-out threatens to obscure the real issue at hand: how to go beyond the piecemeal Affordable Care Act (ACA) and build a truly universal health care system that provides equal, high-quality care to everyone. While many on both the left and right predicted—albeit for different reasons—Obamacare's problems, it would be a mistake to get distracted by what are largely stopgap measures to curb the excesses of the current market-based system. Instead, it is time for constructive new initiatives that steer the current energy around health care reform toward the goal of guaranteeing the right to health care for all. Despite the paranoid visions of conspiracy theorists like [conservative political commentator and radio talk show host] Rush Limbaugh, there is little chance that universal, publicly financed health care will simply emerge automatically from the imaginary Trojan horse of the Affordable Care Act.

In reality, the only thing inevitable about Obamacare is the political wrangling that obfuscates the true challenge ahead. Yet below the radar of the Beltway and media, promising initiatives are surfacing. The best hope for truly universal health care comes from the small state of Vermont, which is on the road to establishing a single-payer-style, publicly financed health care system, after passing the country's first universal health care law in 2011. The innovative people's movement instrumental to achieving this breakthrough has now inspired Healthcare Is a Human Right campaigns in other states across the country. While keeping their eyes on the prize of universal health care, these campaigns are carefully navigating the challenges and opportunities of ACA reforms.

Obamacare's Policy Problems

Clearly, Obamacare's problems cannot simply be ignored or belittled. The list of everything that's wrong with the ACA has grown so long that the media are struggling to keep up. In addition to the high-profile embarrassment of the flawed marketplace website, which triggered a postponement of the on-line small business exchange and may well delay the enforcement of the controversial individual mandate to buy insurance (following the already delayed employer mandate), the president's decision to allow skimpy insurance policies to be reinstated is likely to compound problems in the future. As insurance companies—ever vigilant about their bottom lines—were quick to point out, if younger and healthier people can keep their skimpy coverage outside the exchange, profit-seeking insurers may use "market pressures" as an excuse for raising premiums on people inside the exchange.

The ACA was never designed to provide universal coverage, yet the number of excluded people has increased considerably since the Supreme Court gutted the ACA and made the expansion of Medicaid a state choice.

Moreover, for every person who can "keep their coverage if they like it," there will be many more who won't be able to keep their doctor or hospital, however much they like them. As insurance companies further restrict their networks, cutting even big hospitals out of their policies, the false "choices" offered in a market-based system that treats patients as consumers become abundantly clear: Consumers can choose their coverage, but they can't choose their care.

Using Coverage May Be Hard

Furthermore, whether they'll be able to use their coverage to actually see a doctor—any doctor—depends on the amount of disposable income a person has at hand to satisfy their plan's high deductibles and co-pays. Such cost calculations will increasingly affect not only those in the exchange marketplace, but also those covered by ever-shrinking employer group plans. Employers are set to use Obamacare's "marketplace" emphasis as an excuse for further stratifying their group plans, pushing workers into a privatized shopping mall of highly tiered insurance options within their—presumably non-unionized—workplace.

While all of this is bad news for anyone seeking access to care through coverage via the exchange or their employer, what about the 31 million people projected to remain entirely without insurance? The ACA was never designed to provide universal coverage, yet the number of excluded people has increased considerably since the Supreme Court gutted the ACA and made the expansion of Medicaid a state choice. In a reform predicated on channeling more publicly subsidized "consumers" to private insurance companies, it was primarily the expansion of the public Medicaid program that promised to make the health care system more universal and equitable.

It seems nonsensical to transfer more public money into the coffers of private corporations, thus solidifying the market-based insurance system, when it is this very system that has failed to ensure access to care for all.

Excluding Those with the Most Need

Yet about half the states have opted out, and these are precisely the states in which an expansion is most needed: states with extremely limited Medicaid eligibility, high rates of uninsured people, high levels of poverty, low wages, and skeletal public services. In these states, the ACA is about to leave a gaping hole of 8 million people who will be excluded from both Medicaid and public subsidies in the exchange (which are not available to those below poverty level). At the same time, the ACA will reduce support for public and charity hospitals based on a projected decrease in the number of uninsured people, leaving millions of people with literally nowhere to go for needed care.

This exclusion from health care will have a disproportionate racial impact, as nearly six in ten uninsured African Americans eligible for an expanded Medicaid program live in the opt-out states.

Such clear failures to meet the basic human rights principles of universality and equity put the frenzied focus on Obamacare's website delays into perspective. The ACA, even once fully operational, will have tiers and gaps in its coverage system that segregate lower-income people from the wealthy, and people of color from white people.

Universal, Equitable Health Care Is a Human Right

The ACA's differential impact on poor and rich, and people of color and whites, has entered the public debate perversely through right-wing pundits railing against any potential redistributional effects of a universal health care system that shares risks, costs, and benefits among everyone. Yet the ACA offers no such system; on the contrary, it is precisely the focus on means-tested subsidies in the exchange, and means-tested eligibility for Medicaid, that precludes the unifying appeal a universal program would have. Unless reforms treat health care as a human right and provide it as a public good for all, the politics of competitive individualism, persistent structural racism and decades of warfare against the poor are likely to draw resentment of any public program, even when poor people and people of color have very little to gain.

Advocates for universal, publicly financed health care have long criticized the ACA's approach of using means-tested public subsidies to prop up private insurers. It seems nonsensical to transfer more public money into the coffers of private corporations, thus solidifying the market-based insurance system, when it is this very system that has failed to ensure access to care for all and causes the U.S. to lag behind in key international health indicators.

Yet while a single-payer alternative can marshal most evidence in its support, single payer advocacy has made little progress over the past few decades. Political change is not a matter of having the better argument; it requires building enough people power to overcome the very real ideological and financial power embedded in the existing system. A universal health care community that is divided into ACA supporters and single payer advocates is unlikely to achieve this.

On the Road to Real Change

Vermont's *Healthcare Is a Human Right* campaign, led by the Vermont Workers' Center, has begun to change all this. By building a broad-based people's movement for human rights, the campaign became a strong and unified force with the power to change what was considered politically possible. By focusing on people and their human right to health care, grounded in basic principles rather than technical policy prescriptions, the campaign was able to set the state on a path toward a universal, equitable system that will provide health care as a public good to every Vermont resident. Since 2011, this breakthrough has catalyzed similar campaigns for the human right to health care across the country.

Inspired by Vermont's human rights organizing model, groups in Maine, Maryland, and Pennsylvania studied the lessons learned, picked up the torch and started developing innovative campaigns in their own states. Together with related campaigns on the West Coast, they seek to pave the way for a domino effect of state-based universal health care wins. The *Healthcare Is a Human Right* campaigns build on ACA efforts and draw on single payer arguments where they can, yet their focus is on organizing people to stand up for their rights and demand a truly universal and equitable health care system.

4

Millions of Poor Are Left Uncovered by Health Law

Sabrina Tavernise and Robert Gebeloff

Sabrina Tavernise and Robert Gebeloff are staff writers for The New York Times.

When the US Supreme Court upheld the constitutionality of the Affordable Care Act (ACA) in 2012, its decision also maintained that individual states could opt out of expanding their Medicaid medical insurance programs for the poor as part of the ACA. Twenty-six states initially refused to expand Medicaid, effectively leaving eight million of the country's poorest people without health coverage and without the eligibility to obtain it. Ironically, many of these "opt-out" states have the largest concentrations of poor, uninsured adults to begin with. Impoverished communities of color are especially hard hit by the coverage disparity because they make up a large percentage of the populations in these states. In a further irony, individuals with incomes that are higher than Medicaid eligibility would now qualify for federal subsidies to purchase coverage from private insurance companies, while their poorer counterparts do not qualify for any coverage at all.

Editor's Note: Since this viewpoint was written, several more states have decided to participate in the Medicaid expansion under the Affordable Care Act, and several others are debating the issue.

A sweeping national effort to extend health coverage to millions of Americans will leave out two-thirds of the poor blacks and single mothers and more than half of the low-wage workers who do not have insurance, the very kinds of people that the program was intended to help, according to an analysis of census data by *The New York Times.*

Because they live in states largely controlled by Republicans that have declined to participate in a vast expansion of Medicaid, the medical insurance program for the poor, they are among the eight million Americans who are impoverished, uninsured and ineligible for help. The federal government will pay for the expansion through 2016 and no less than 90 percent of costs in later years.

Those excluded will be stranded without insurance, stuck between people with slightly higher incomes who will qualify for federal subsidies on the new health exchanges that went live this week [October 2013], and those who are poor enough to qualify for Medicaid in its current form, which has income ceilings as low as $11 a day in some states.

People shopping for insurance on the health exchanges are already discovering this bitter twist.

"How can somebody in poverty not be eligible for subsidies?" an unemployed health care worker in Virginia asked through tears. The woman, who identified herself only as Robin L. because she does not want potential employers to know she is down on her luck, thought she had run into a computer problem when she went online Tuesday [October 1, 2013] and learned she would not qualify.

At 55, she has high blood pressure, and she had been waiting for the law to take effect so she could get coverage. Before she lost her job and her house and had to move in with her brother in Virginia, she lived in Maryland, a state that is expanding Medicaid. "Would I go back there?" she asked. "It might involve me living in my car. I don't know. I might consider it."

The 26 states that have rejected the Medicaid expansion are home to about half of the country's population, but about 68 percent of poor, uninsured blacks and single mothers. About 60 percent of the country's uninsured working poor are in those states. Among those excluded are about 435,000 cashiers, 341,000 cooks and 253,000 nurses' aides.

Every state in the Deep South, with the exception of Arkansas, has rejected the [Medicaid] expansion.

"The irony is that these states that are rejecting Medicaid expansion—many of them Southern—are the very places where the concentration of poverty and lack of health insurance are the most acute," said Dr. H. Jack Geiger, a founder of the community health center model. "It is their populations that have the highest burden of illness and costs to the entire health care system."

Race Becomes a Factor

The disproportionate impact on poor blacks introduces the prickly issue of race into the already politically charged atmosphere around the health care law. Race was rarely, if ever, mentioned in the state-level debates about the Medicaid expansion. But the issue courses just below the surface, civil rights leaders say, pointing to the pattern of exclusion.

Every state in the Deep South, with the exception of Arkansas, has rejected the expansion. Opponents of the expansion say they are against it on exclusively economic grounds, and that the demographics of the South—with its large share of poor blacks—make it easy to say race is an issue when it is not.

In Mississippi, Republican leaders note that a large share of people in the state are on Medicaid already, and that, with an expansion, about a third of the state would have been insured through the program. Even supporters of the health law say that eventually covering 10 percent of that cost would have been onerous for a predominantly rural state with a modest tax base.

Those [states] that opted not to [expand Medicaid] leave about eight million uninsured people who live in poverty ($19,530 for a family of three) without any assistance at all.

"Any additional cost in Medicaid is going to be too much," said State Senator Chris McDaniel, a Republican, who opposes expansion.

The law was written to require all Americans to have health coverage. For lower and middle-income earners, there are subsidies on the new health exchanges to help them afford insurance. An expanded Medicaid program was intended to cover the poorest. In all, about 30 million uninsured Americans were to have become eligible for financial help.

Supreme Court Allowed Loophole for States

But the Supreme Court's ruling on the health care law last year, while upholding it, allowed states to choose whether to expand Medicaid. Those that opted not to leave about eight million uninsured people who live in poverty ($19,530 for a family of three) without any assistance at all.

Poor people excluded from the Medicaid expansion will not be subject to fines for lacking coverage. In all, about 14 million eligible Americans are uninsured and living in poverty, the *Times* analysis found.

The federal government provided the tally of how many states were not expanding Medicaid for the first time on Tuesday [October 1, 2013]. It included states like New Hampshire, Ohio, Pennsylvania and Tennessee that might still decide to expand Medicaid before coverage takes effect in January

[2014]. If those states go forward, the number would change, but the trends that emerged in the analysis would be similar.

Mississippi has the largest percentage of poor and uninsured people in the country—13 percent. Willie Charles Carter, an unemployed 53-year-old whose most recent job was as a maintenance worker at a public school, has had problems with his leg since surgery last year.

His income is below Mississippi's ceiling for Medicaid—which is about $3,000 a year—but he has no dependent children, so he does not qualify. And his income is too low to make him eligible for subsidies on the federal health exchange.

"You got to be almost dead before you can get Medicaid in Mississippi," he said.

He does not know what he will do when the clinic where he goes for medical care, the Good Samaritan Health Center in Greenville, closes next month because of lack of funding.

"I'm scared all the time," he said. "I just walk around here with faith in God to take care of me."

Less Generous Safety Nets

The states that did not expand Medicaid have less generous safety nets: For adults with children, the median income limit for Medicaid is just under half of the federal poverty level—or about $5,600 a year for an individual—while in states that are expanding, it is above the poverty line, or about $12,200, according to the Kaiser Family Foundation. There is little or no coverage of childless adults in the states not expanding, Kaiser said.

The New York Times analysis excluded immigrants in the country illegally and those foreign-born residents who would not be eligible for benefits under Medicaid expansion. It included people who are uninsured even though they qualify for Medicaid in its current form.

Blacks are disproportionately affected, largely because more of them are poor and living in Southern states. In all, 6 out of

10 blacks live in the states not expanding Medicaid. In Mississippi, 56 percent of all poor and uninsured adults are black, though they account for just 38 percent of the population.

Dr. Aaron Shirley, a physician who has worked for better health care for blacks in Mississippi, said that the history of segregation and violence against blacks still informs the way people see one another, particularly in the South, making some whites reluctant to support programs that they believe benefit blacks.

The decision not to expand Medicaid will also hit the working poor.

That is compounded by the country's rapidly changing demographics, Dr. Geiger said, in which minorities will eventually become a majority, a pattern that has produced a profound cultural unease, particularly when it has collided with economic insecurity.

Dr. Shirley said: "If you look at the history of Mississippi, politicians have used race to oppose minimum wage, Head Start, all these social programs. It's a tactic that appeals to people who would rather suffer themselves than see a black person benefit."

Opponents Say Race Isn't a Factor

Opponents of the expansion bristled at the suggestion that race had anything to do with their position. State Senator Giles Ward of Mississippi, a Republican, called the idea that race was a factor "preposterous," and said that with the demographics of the South—large shares of poor people and, in particular, poor blacks—"you can argue pretty much any way you want."

The decision not to expand Medicaid will also hit the working poor. Claretha Briscoe earns just under $11,000 a year making fried chicken and other fast food at a convenience store in Hollandale, Miss., too much to qualify for Medicaid but not enough to get subsidies on the new health exchange. She had a heart attack in 2002 that a local hospital treated as part of its charity care program.

"I skip months on my blood pressure pills," said Ms. Briscoe, 48, who visited the Good Samaritan Health Center last week because she was having chest pains. "I buy them when I can afford them."

About half of poor and uninsured Hispanics live in states that are expanding Medicaid. But Texas, which has a large Hispanic population, rejected the expansion. Gladys Arbila, a housekeeper in Houston who earns $17,000 a year and supports two children, is under the poverty line and therefore not eligible for new subsidies. But she makes too much to qualify for Medicaid under the state's rules. She recently spent 36 hours waiting in the emergency room for a searing pain in her back.

"We came to this country, and we are legal and we work really hard," said Ms. Arbila, 45, who immigrated to the United States 12 years ago, and whose son is a soldier in Afghanistan. "Why we don't have the same opportunities as the others?"

5

Obamacare: What If Not Enough Young, Healthy People Enroll?

Linda Feldmann

Linda Feldmann is chief political correspondent for The Christian Science Monitor *newspaper.*

The success of the Affordable Care Act (ACA) depends on enough young, healthy people enrolling in the program in order to offset the health-care expenses incurred by older participants who are likely to have more health problems and be more frequent consumers of health services. This model of shared risk is the reason that the ACA includes a mandate that requires all Americans to have insurance. If only old and sick people bought insurance and participated, the program would not be able to pay for all of their care and it would cause premiums to skyrocket. Since health plan enrollment under the ACA is still in its initial phases, only time will tell whether young people have enrolled in sufficient numbers to allow the program to function efficiently. The ACA has several safeguards built in to reduce risk if the enrollment numbers end up unbalanced and are skewed toward higher-cost enrollees.

Young adults were there for Barack Obama both times he ran for president. Now he needs them more than ever—to buy health insurance.

Linda Feldmann, "Obamacare: What If Not Enough Young, Healthy People Enroll?" *The Christian Science Monitor*, December 5, 2013. Copyright © 2013 by Christian Science Monitor. All rights reserved. Reproduced by permission.

But it's not clear they'll deliver. A poll released this week by Harvard's Institute of Politics on American "Millennials"—those aged 18 to 29—bore the bad news: A majority (56 percent) of Millennials disapprove of the Affordable Care Act (ACA), and only 29 percent of uninsured people in that age group plan to buy coverage via HealthCare.gov or a state-run exchange.

If the individual insurance market is to work, a significant percentage of young, healthy people need to pay into the system. The reason is that they are effectively subsidizing the older enrollees—those in the 50-to-64 age band, who on average are less healthy than the younger group.

"So for every old person you get, you want to get some young people in as well to help cover your costs, on average," says Larry Levitt, a senior vice president at the Kaiser Family Foundation.

The worst-case scenario for Obamacare would be a "death spiral" in which not enough healthy people sign up, meaning insurance companies have mostly high-cost customers on their plans. The result would be drastically higher premiums that threaten the long-term viability of the program.

How Many Young Enrollees Does Obamacare Need?

It has long been reported that the Obama administration aimed to enroll 7 million people in the new online exchanges for 2014, including 2.7 million people between the ages of 18 and 34, or 38.5 percent of the total. When asked, an administration official involved in health policy would only say that there needs to be a "mix" of people of all ages in the insurance pool. No numbers or percentages.

For 18- to 34-year-olds, the rule of thumb is to enroll them at roughly the proportion represented in the enrollee population as a whole. They represent about one-third of the population that is between 18 and 64. At 65, people can enroll in Medicare.

Health insurance premiums vary by age, but the variation is limited under the ACA to a ratio of 3 to 1. So someone who's 64 can be charged only three times someone who's 21. That's less than the variation that exists in the individual market today, which is typically more in the range of 5 to 1.

What Happens If Not Enough Young People Sign Up?

That's the gazillion-dollar question. First, it depends on the size of the shortfall of young enrollees.

David Axene, a fellow at the Society of Actuaries, says he would start to worry if the 18- to 34-year-old age group was underrepresented by 15 to 20 percent.

"That's when I would start to say that it's serious," he says.

Early indications are that enrollment is skewing toward older people.

If the final percentage of young people was in the 20 percent range, for example, "that would result in a rather significant increase in premium rates above and beyond inflation to make up for that loss."

And add to that concerns about "health status selection"—that is, where healthy people opt out of insurance.

What Do the Numbers Look Like So Far?

The Obama administration has not yet released demographic information on enrollees yet, but is expected to in mid-December, in its monthly report on enrollment.

Early indications are that enrollment is skewing toward older people. Two weeks ago, the California exchange reported that in October, only 23 percent of enrollees were age 18 to 34, while 56 percent were in the 45-to-64 category.

The information is "too sporadic to draw conclusions, but it appears it's an older population than what some [insurers] had assumed," says Mr. Axene of the Society of Actuaries.

Mr. Levitt read the California numbers positively.

"What really matters is who's enrolled as of March 31," the last day of open enrollment for 2014, Levitt says. "So I took the California numbers as encouraging, because they were further along among young people than I would have expected."

When We Do Have Numbers, How Should We Interpret Them?

First, one must consider each state separately, because insurance is pooled at the state level.

"Enrolling a young person in California isn't going to help you in Texas," says Levitt. "You could end up in a situation where some states have very balanced risk pools and other states don't, depending on how effective the outreach."

Also, Levitt notes, one must look at everyone in the individual market in each state, not just those enrolling through the exchanges. People can buy insurance outside the exchanges, but if they do, they are not eligible for a federal subsidy.

What About Adult Children Under the Age of 26?

Under the ACA, people under the age of 26 are allowed to stay on their parents' health plan. For many young adults, it's the cheapest way to get covered. As of June 2013, 3.1 million people had taken up this option. But it also takes them out of the individual market, so they're not helping to offset the costs of older enrollees.

If the Market Ends Up Imbalanced, How Does Obamacare Address That?

The ACA provides for what are called the "three R's"— reinsurance, risk corridors, and risk adjustment. Reinsurance is a pot of money, funded by a tax on every health plan, that helps insurers cover the costs of expensive claims. Under a recent rule change, reinsurance would pay 80 percent of the cost of claims over $45,000, down from $60,000. The ceiling is $250,000.

The program called risk corridors, available only to insurers on the new exchanges, exists to even out premiums. If an insurer takes in more than it ends up needing, it gives some of the excess to the government. If its premiums end up being too low, the government will cover some of the losses.

The risk adjustment program takes money from insurers that had healthier-than-average customers and gives it to insurers with more-expensive customers. That removes the incentive by insurers to recruit only healthy customers.

The first two risk mitigation programs are in effect for three years, 2014 to 2016. Risk adjustment is permanent.

6

The Affordable Care Act Will Benefit Rich and Poor Alike

Froma Harrop

Froma Harrop is a nationally syndicated columnist who previously reported on business for Reuters and was a financial editor for the New York Times News Service.

The Affordable Care Act (ACA) has gotten a lot of attention for its bungled rollout and other difficulties, but a key point has been lost among all the chatter: the act is already fulfilling one of its key purposes by slowing health-care spending. The prices for health-care services have also slowed their climb. That translates to more money in taxpayers' pockets as federal and state governments are able to cut their projected spending on health care. These changes are due to the reforms in the ACA, such as rewarding providers for providing good care rather than seeing large numbers of patients, and penalizing hospitals that have high readmission rates. The wealthy will benefit from the ACA just as much as the poor and middle class because when spending goes down, so do taxes. Overall, the reforms in the ACA will reduce the federal deficit by more than $100 billion through 2022, which is good for taxpayers at all income levels.

During the botched rollout of the Affordable Care Act, it's been hard to defend the law, much less to call it "great." But great it is—for the American economy and for the American people, rich ones included.

The program has already succeeded in one of its key back-breaking missions: to curb the exploding costs of health care. The president's Council of Economic Advisers issued a report this month [November 2013] containing lots of good news on that front.

Since Obamacare was passed in 2010, the growth in health care spending has slowed to the lowest rate on record for any three-year period since 1965. "If half the recent slowdown in spending can be sustained," the report says, "health care spending a decade from now will be about $1,400 per person lower than if growth returned to its 2000–2007 trend."

The authors further note that the benefit will go to workers in the form of fatter paychecks and to taxpayers as federal and state governments cut projected spending on health care. Another plus would be more jobs as employers feel less burdened by the cost of covering their workers.

Reducing Health Care Costs

What about the recession? One may reasonably ask whether the economic downturn was responsible for cutting the growth rates of medical spending. Yes, but not by much, the authors respond.

They note that the slowdown has persisted well beyond the end of the recession. Very importantly, it also applied to Medicare, a government program whose elderly beneficiaries are more insulated from a weak job market. And the growth in *prices* for health services (different from total spending) has eased significantly.

Here's how the health care reforms did it:

- They reduced the overpayments to private insurers' Medicare Advantage plans and the price increases for providers.

- They're promoting new payment models, whereby medical providers are being financially rewarded for giving good care in an efficient manner. Under the old setup, providers could enhance their incomes by pumping up the volume of visits, tests and other services.

The reforms encourage the growth of "accountable care organizations." The more efficiently these groups of medical providers operate the more money they get to keep.

The Congressional Budget Office ... expects the reforms overall to reduce the deficit by more than $100 billion from 2013 to 2022.

- Hospitals with high readmission rates are penalized. This is also a quality issue for Medicare beneficiaries, who are often discharged with inadequate planning for post-hospital care. Under a perverse set of incentives, hospitals were making more money when elderly patients returned. The taxpayers, of course, picked up the bills.

- Changes in Medicare should spill over into the private sector, generating even more savings. Medicare's payment structure is often the starting point in negotiations between private insurers and medical providers.

Taxes Rise with Spending

What about the rich? All this conservative talk about Obamacare's "redistributing" wealth to the less well-off ignores this reality: Every time medical spending rises, so do the taxes (of those who pay income tax) and the premiums for those who buy their own coverage.

I mean, who do you think has been paying for all those uninsured people showing up at expensive hospital emergency rooms for free care?

For those worried about federal deficits, here are some encouraging numbers, courtesy of the Affordable Care Act: The Congressional Budget Office recently cut its projected Medicare and Medicaid spending in 2020 by $147 billion. It expects the reforms overall to reduce the deficit by more than $100 billion from 2013 to 2022.

All this great stuff has been obscured by the bungled launch of the federal government's HealthCare.gov website. Once it is up and running, the conversation should turn in a more positive direction. Those who read the advisers' report won't have to wait that long. Google "Council of Economic Advisers" for a copy.

7

The Affordable Care Act Will Help Contain Health-Care Costs

Stephen Zuckerman and John Holahan

Stephen Zuckerman is a senior fellow and John Holahan is the director of the Health Policy Research Center at the Urban Institute, a nonprofit, nonpartisan policy research and educational center that examines the nation's social, economic, and governance problems.

Critics have argued that the Affordable Care Act (ACA) does not address the growing costs of health care, but in fact the ACA puts health-care costs in check in several different ways. The health insurance exchanges set up under the Act are based on the market-based strategy of "managed competition," which helps keep costs down through incentives for competition. Additionally, an overhaul of existing Medicare reimbursements and cost-shifting in that system will slow ballooning expenditures. The act also discourages health-care cost inflation by levying an excise tax on high-cost employer-sponsored insurance plans that cost more than an established maximum. Finally, a variety of mechanisms designed to improve efficiency and reduce waste will help hold costs down. These measures and others are already reducing the projections of future health expenditures.

Stephen Zuckerman and John Holahan, "Despite Criticism, The Affordable Care Act Does Much to Contain Health Care Costs," Urban.org, *Urban Institute*, October 2012.

Critics of the Affordable Care Act (ACA) have argued that the law fails to address health care cost growth. They allege that though Americans rank concerns about access and costs as the two major problems with the health care system, the legislation largely ignores the cost issue, focusing instead on coverage for the uninsured. Many who make this argument tend to believe that medical malpractice is the major cost driver and since the legislation gave malpractice little attention, the law has no meaningful cost containment. While malpractice may be a cost driver to be considered, it is clear that it is not the only factor. As we outline in this brief, there are many components of the Affordable Care Act that are designed to contain costs. Some of these are expected to lower the rate of growth in spending, particularly in Medicare. Others are more experimental and hold promise to fundamentally change the way health care is delivered, improving quality and making the system more efficient.

It appears from Centers for Medicare & Medicaid Services (CMS) actuaries and Congressional Budget Office (CBO) projections that the rate of growth in health care spending has already slowed, in part because of the economy, but also because of provisions of the Affordable Care Act. In this brief we discuss the managed competition framework embedded in health insurance exchanges, the Medicare provider payment cuts, the excise tax on high cost health insurance plans and several other proposals designed to slow cost growth.

Competition in Exchanges

Managed competition has been proposed for many years as a market-oriented strategy for containing health care cost growth. Under the ACA, health insurance exchanges will be developed in each state to facilitate a competitive marketplace for the purchase of private insurance coverage by nonelderly individuals/families and small employers (100 or fewer employees). Among other roles, the exchanges will certify qualified health plans, contract with insurance carriers, determine eligibility for financial subsidies for exchange plans or Medicaid, distribute subsidies, provide consumer-friendly information to help purchasers compare plans, and facilitate enrollment. Qualified individuals with incomes below 400 percent of the federal poverty level (FPL) (generally, legal residents without affordable employer-sponsored insurance offers and who are not eligible for public insurance programs) will be eligible for federally financed subsidies that lower the cost of purchasing nongroup health insurance in the exchange. The structure of the exchanges and the approach used to benchmark the amount of the premium subsidies should engender strong competitive pressures among insurers and provide incentives for enrollees to select lower-cost plans.

The exchange structure and the insurance regulation reforms included in the ACA should serve to direct insurers toward increasing the efficiency of providing care, thus lowering premium prices and increasing market share.

Insurers providing small group and nongroup coverage in or out of the exchanges will only be allowed to offer plans that fit into four tiers of actuarial value (AV)—bronze (60 percent AV), silver (70 percent AV), gold (80 percent AV), and platinum plans (90 percent AV)—with each level differing primarily on cost-sharing requirements, as all will be required to offer the essential benefits as defined by the Department of Health and Human Services. Within each AV tier, multiple insurers can offer products. Subsidies will be tied to the premiums of the second lowest cost silver plan offered in the area. Individuals who want a silver plan with a premium in excess of this benchmark, or a gold or platinum plan, will have to pay the full marginal cost of such a plan. Those with incomes below 250 percent FPL will also qualify for federal cost-sharing subsidies.

Competition Incentives

In theory, requiring enrollees to pay the full difference between higher-cost plans and the benchmark plan should lead to strong competition among insurers. Insurers will compete on network adequacy, service, and price. There will be risk adjustment to compensate insurers who get a bad mix of risks. This structure generally meets the criteria for managed competition. Individuals will have to pay extra premiums or can be expected to gravitate toward less expensive plans, those that have limited networks, those that are effective at managing care, and those using less costly providers. Individuals would also be expected to have plans with reasonably high deductibles and more cost-sharing.

Payment reductions [in Medicare] will mean hospitals will either have to adjust their expenses or, if they can, increase prices to other payers.

How much this would affect health care spending is uncertain. Reduced variation in the types of plans offered in the small-group and nongroup markets, and consumer information produced by exchanges to assist individuals and groups in becoming more effective purchasers will also increase competitive pressures in these markets. Currently, these markets are often characterized by tremendous variation in plan options, but very limited information is made available *a priori* to potential consumers about the coverage they may be purchasing. Insurers are often more focused on strategies for gaining favorable risk selection than they are in competing based on price and quality. The exchange structure and the insurance regulation reforms included in the ACA should serve to direct insurers toward increasing the efficiency of providing care, thus lowering premium prices and increasing market share.

Having large numbers of insurers is not necessarily a blessing in the health care market if this means they each lack the market power needed to get a good deal from providers. In some markets a single insurer may be so dominant that it is hard for others to enter because they don't have the market share to allow them to effectively negotiate with providers. An additional problem with competition in exchanges is that it is limited to the people in individual and small group markets who are enrolled in exchange plans. By our estimates, there will be about 45 million people entering either into the nongroup exchanges or the Small Business Health Options (SHOP) exchanges. Of course, the plans outside the exchanges will to some degree be competing with the plans inside, and if the plans inside are able to control health care costs more successfully, more people will gravitate toward purchasing coverage in the exchange, even without subsidies. Thus, there is likely to be some spillover to the outside market.

Medicare Payment Reductions

A second major cost containment feature of the ACA is the reduction in annual market-based updates for Medicare payment rates to hospitals, skilled nursing facilities, home health agencies, and hospices, as well as reductions in Medicare disproportionate share payments and payments to Medicare Advantage plans. The lower provider updates are intended to reflect or encourage greater productivity in these sectors. The CMS actuaries estimate that these provisions will have lowered the rate of growth in Medicare by 1 percent per year, or by more than 10 percent over 10 years.

For skilled nursing facilities, home health agencies, and hospices, Medicare is the dominant payer and these providers have no other payers that can be expected to provide adequate cross-subsidies. As such, they will need to adjust their cost structures to be consistent with Medicare payments. However, the effects of constraining hospital inpatient updates may be more complicated, given the market power of many hospitals. A recent study found that 88 percent of large metropolitan areas are considered to have highly concentrated hospital markets, contributing to the rapid growth in health care costs. A number of studies have shown that private hospital rates are higher in more concentrated markets, where it is difficult for private insurers to effectively negotiate or control rates. But, Medicare's administered pricing system sets rates for diagnostic related groups with adjustments for geography, teaching and other factors; the market power of hospitals is not a factor.

The largest effect of the new excise tax is predicted to be a shift in compensation away from health insurance benefits, toward wages.

Cost Shifting

Medicare is the largest payer for hospitals, and payment reductions will mean hospitals will either have to adjust their expenses or, if they can, increase prices to other payers. If hospitals are able to shift costs to their private payers because of market power, hospital expenses will increase despite Medicare restraints. If they cannot shift costs on to private payers, they will need to control expenses. The Medicare Payment Advisory Commission (MedPAC) recently showed that, in areas where insurers have more market power over hospitals, there is more financial pressure and hospital expenses are lower, and Medicare payments appear to be adequate. Conversely, they found that where hospitals have strong market power relative to insurers, hospital expenses are higher and Medicare payments do not cover them. The MedPAC results suggest that cost shifting can only occur where there are weak payers and strong providers.

A 2004 study by Robinson foreshadowed these MedPAC results: In competitive provider markets, hospitals could not cost shift and thus controlled costs, while the reverse was true in concentrated markets. Another recent study also confirms the MedPAC findings, concluding that on average providers shift only 21 cents for each dollar lost on Medicare; this implies that they cannot or do not shift the other 79 cents. Thus, the efforts of the ACA to reduce Medicare payments should reduce hospital costs in many markets, but not all.

Excise Tax on High-Cost Employer-Sponsored Insurance Plans

Beginning in 2018, the ACA will impose a new 40 percent excise tax on employer-sponsored plans costing more than a threshold premium level. The amount of the tax will be computed by the insurance carriers and added into the premium paid by those purchasing the insurance, thereby increasing the purchase price of coverage. The intent of this provision is to reduce the incentive for employers to provide more comprehensive plans than this threshold employer-based insurance plan. This approach is an attempt to address perverse incentives associated with the income tax exclusion for employer-paid insurance, that increases in value with premiums. The threshold premium level for single coverage will be $10,200 in 2018; the level for policies covering more than one person will be $27,500 that year.

The thresholds used in 2018 will be adjusted upward if premium growth in the Blue Cross Blue Shield standard option under the Federal Employees Health Benefits Plan grows faster than an average of about 5.6 percent per year between 2010 and 2018. The thresholds will also be adjusted based on employers' workforce age and gender composition. The law also increases the thresholds for workers and retirees covered under employer plans in certain high-risk industries (e.g., police officers, firefighters, first responders, construction workers, agricultural workers, and others); their threshold for single coverage is increased by $1,650 and for other coverage by

$3,450 in 2018. The threshold premium levels will increase each year after 2020 by the consumer price index for urban consumers (CPI-U). Since health care costs and premiums will likely grow faster than the CPI, the threshold will become increasingly binding overtime.

Using Fewer Health Services

The largest effect of the new excise tax is predicted to be a shift in compensation away from health insurance benefits, toward wages as a consequence of some employers purchasing less comprehensive health insurance for their workers. This implies a consequent reduction in the utilization of health care services when these employees are faced with higher deductibles, larger co-payments, lower out-of-pocket limits, and possibly fewer covered benefits.

> *Another provision [of the ACA] establishes an Independent Payment Advisory Board that would make recommendations for payment cuts if Medicare expenditures per enrollee grow faster than GDP plus .5 percent.*

The magnitude of the savings in health expenditures resulting from higher out-of-pocket costs is difficult to quantify, even though there is an extensive literature related to the effects of cost-sharing on hearth expenditures. This literature has been summarized and analyzed most recently in a synthesis by Katherine Swartz. The most comprehensive analyses of the effects of cost-sharing on spending were done using the results of the Rand Health Insurance Experiment (HIE) in the 1970s. While the structure of health insurance policies and patterns of use and spending in health care have changed significantly since then, those studies are still instructive. HIE researchers found that higher cost-sharing does reduce health care utilization, but only patient-initiated health care spending. Once a patient was under the care of a physician, the use of medical care did not vary as a function of cost-sharing, suggesting that the physician was directing medical use decisions at that point, not the patient.

Thus, it seems that increased cost-sharing will lead those with the lowest health care needs to forego patient-initiated spending. This, combined with the strongly skewed distribution of health care spending (i.e., only 10 percent of the population accounts for 65 percent of total spending), means that the excise tax on its own is not likely to achieve significant health savings—at least initially. However, by using the CPI to update the tax threshold, more and more plans will get pushed into the taxable range and the impact of the tax could get stronger. Even though the highest spenders may still be relatively unaffected, because they are seriously ill and most of their expenditures are above out-of-pocket limits in insurance plans, recent analysis suggests that moderate limits on the tax exclusion (well short of eliminating it) can cause a shift to less generous coverage that could produce savings on the order of 1.5 percent of National Health Expenditures. This would be a significant effect within the range of alternative cost containment policy options.

Other Provisions

There are a number of other provisions in the ACA that have the potential to contain costs. The ACA authorizes the establishment of a nonprofit corporation, the Patient-Centered Outcomes Research Institute, to conduct and broadly disseminate comparative-effectiveness research. This research effort is intended to inform "patients, clinicians, purchasers, and policy-makers in making informed health decisions" regarding relative health outcomes, clinical effectiveness, and appropriateness of medical treatments and services. The law outlines the factors for the new Institute to use in setting research priorities, including disease incidence, prevalence, and burden in the United States (particularly emphasizing chronic conditions; gaps in evidence, practice variations and health disparities; potential for improving patient health, well-being, and the quality of care; and the effect on national health expenditures.)

The law allows for the research produced by the Institute to be used in making coverage, reimbursement, and incentive decisions under the Medicare program, although a number of safeguards are put in place. For example, the Secretary of Health and Human Services (HHS) is prohibited from denying coverage of services or items "solely on the basis of comparative clinical effectiveness research," and the law emphasizes that the research findings are not to be construed as mandates for coverage and reimbursement decisions. Moreover, the analytical information collected by the Institute may not be used for Medicare reimbursement and coverage decisions "in a manner that treats extending the life of an elderly, disabled, or terminally ill individual as of lower value than extending the life of an individual who is younger, nondisabled, or not terminally ill."

Another provision establishes an Independent Payment Advisory Board that would make recommendations for payment cuts if Medicare expenditures per enrollee grow faster than GDP [gross domestic product] plus .5 percent. There are limits on the policies and providers affected. For example, it may not recommend policies that would change eligibility and beneficiary cost sharing or increase revenues. In addition hospitals and hospices could not be affected until 2020.

Accountable Care Organizations

The ACA also allows for the establishment of Accountable Care Organizations (ACO), which would be designed to take responsibility for care of patients, coordinate care, and improve efficiency. The intent is to provide financial incentives to both improve quality and reduce costs. An expenditure target for the ACO would be established. If costs for the designated population could be provided at a lower cost, the ACO would share the savings with Medicare.

The Affordable Care Act also includes provisions for reducing payments to hospitals with high levels of readmissions. Specifically, starting in 2013, Medicare payments will be reduced for hospitals with high rates of potentially preventable readmissions, initially for three conditions: acute myocardial infarction, heart failure, and pneumonia. The hospital's actual readmission rate for these conditions will be compared to its expected readmission rate, and the hospital will be subject to a reduction in Medicare payment for excess readmissions.

Other features in the ACA that also could save money are the provisions that affect payments to insurance companies.

The ACA also establishes pilot programs for Medicare to experiment with bundled payments. The focus would be on ten episodes, determined by the secretary of HHS. Bundled payments will replace the discrete payments for each service/provider with a global payment for some or all providers and services related to a particular episode or condition. In the context of acute and procedural episodes (e.g. a hip replacement) a bundled payment could include reimbursement for an outpatient or inpatient episode and related care provided in other settings for a specific interval of time. A bundled payment for a chronic condition would cover all care related to that condition for specified period (e.g. twelve months). The intent is that bundled payments would allow hospitals and other providers more flexibility in allocating resources, and give them opportunities to share savings from their efforts to reduce complications and readmissions.

CMS already has a new office to improve the coordination of care between Medicare and Medicaid for dual eligibles, a population that accounts for about 15 percent of U.S. health spending. Although there have been studies that failed to show savings from care coordination, more recent approaches seem to have more potential for cost savings. Successful programs include interventions targeted at those most likely to benefit. These often rely on nurse and primary care physician teams to engage patients and their families, get providers access to timely information on hospital admissions and emergency room visits, encourage close interaction between care coordinators and primary care physicians, and place an emphasis on teaching self-management skills. Even small reductions, in percentage terms, in spending on dual eligibles would yield large dollar savings.

Other features in the ACA that also could save money are the provisions that affect payments to insurance companies. These include minimum loss ratios for plans selling in the individual and small group markets, requirements that states undertake review of insurer rate filings and the opportunities to adopt an active purchasing model in the exchanges. Exchanges could use the power provided by the ACA to exclude plans from participating based on price or premium growth, i.e., negotiating aggressively with insurers. Because a considerable amount of data collection authority has been provided to the HHS Secretary under the ACA, exchanges should be much better informed of the underlying costs driving price increases, allowing them to be effective negotiators to limit insurer rate increases.

ACA Employs Varied Cost Solutions

It is simply not correct to say that the Affordable Care Act ignores cost containment. Given the urgency of containing the high level of health care spending in the United States, the ACA attacks the problem through a large number of different provisions related to public and private insurance. Prior experience shows some of these will contain cost growth, while others are more experimental but offer promise. Many policy options have been studied in recent years and although some of these made their way into the ACA, it is clear that more could be done.

While more could and perhaps should have been done in the Affordable Care Act, it is simply not accurate to argue that the law's cost containment provisions are weak or non-existent.

One area that is often cited as a major driver of excessive health care spending is medical malpractice and its impact of defensive medicine, i.e. providing marginal services to be prepared to defend against a potential lawsuit. Earlier analyses suggest that some savings could be achieved with medical malpractice reform. [Researchers M.M.] Mello et al. concluded that the medical liability system accounts for 2.4 percent of health care spending. Caps on non-economic damages have been shown to have some effect on medical malpractice premiums paid by physicians and hospitals, though care needs to be taken in the design of such caps. CBO has estimated that a $250,000 cap on non-economic damages would result in savings of about 0.3 to 0.4 percent of national health spending. If defensive medicine could be reduced, more could be saved. The upper bound seems to be around 1 percent of national health expenditures, but only if the care that is now provided for defensive reasons is eliminated and not continued in the name of "good and careful" medicine.

Other measures that would bring down health care costs (more than those already implemented) would be stronger limits on the exclusion of employer sponsored health insurance premiums from income and payroll taxes and direct controls over provider payment rates, possibly as part of global budgets. Neither of these seems politically tenable at the moment and, in all likelihood, the best chance at cost containment over the next few years would be to allow the myriad provisions contained in the ACA a chance to have some effect.

These measures, and a variety of other factors, are already reducing projections of future health expenditures. The CMS actuaries recently projected health expenditures to increase by only one percentage point above GDP growth. They cite the shift to high deductibles in private insurance plans and the development of fewer blockbuster drugs, the adoption of tiered formulas, and greater use of generic drugs. But the actuaries also cite mandated reductions in Medicare fee-for-service rates, lower payments to Medicare Advantage plans, a shift of coverage from employer plans to Medicaid and health insurance exchanges, and the excise tax on high cost plan as reasons to expect lower health spending per capita. For example, Medicare payments per capita are now projected to increase at 3.1 percent per year over the next decade (or 3.8 percent with a fix to the physician payment Sustainable Growth Rate formula), still lower than the projected increase in GDP per capita. While more could and perhaps should have been done in the Affordable Care Act, it is simply not accurate to argue that the law's cost containment provisions are weak or non-existent.

8

Insurance Racket

Andrew Stiles

Andrew Stiles is a political reporter for National Review Online.

The Affordable Care Act (ACA) has been touted as a boon for consumers, but in reality it is a boondoggle for insurers, because not only are individuals now required to buy specific products from private companies (health insurance) but also to subsidize the arrangement as taxpayers. The biggest winners in President Barack Obama's signature health-care reform bill are the insurance companies themselves, without whom the law could not even exist. Not only will the insurance industry garner millions of dollars directly from consumers who purchase new insurance policies, but it will also pocket half a trillion dollars that the government will pay to subsidize the purchase of health-care policies under the ACA. The act also contains built-in taxpayer bailout protections for insurance companies should the venture not prove to be as lucrative as initially expected.

Insurance-company CEOs met with President Obama at the White House on Friday for what presumably was an awkward conversation about the latest wrinkle in their close four-year relationship.

The administrative "fix" to Obamacare is less a substantive policy solution than an effort to shift public outrage over the president's "incorrect promise" away from vulnerable Democrats and onto the very insurance companies whose cooperation is vital to the law's success.

The next several weeks will provide a key test for a complicated relationship dating back to 2009, when the health-insurance industry became an early backer of the Obama administration's reform effort—somewhat ironically, given the relentless public flogging they received in that fight from the president and his Democratic allies.

But by coming to the table and playing nice—and spending millions of dollars to lobby lawmakers—the insurance industry managed to secure a fairly lucrative arrangement. Millions of Americans would be compelled by law to purchase their products. The federal government would pony up almost half a trillion dollars of taxpayer money to subsidize the purchase of health insurance, which will go straight into insurers' pockets. On top of that, if the law worked, many of those government-mandated customers would be ideal clients—young, healthy people unlikely to require expensive care and insurance-company payments.

"Their interests are aligned with our interests in terms of wanting to enroll targeted populations," a senior White House official told *Politico* last week. "It is not that we will agree with everything now either, but I would say for some time now there has been a collaboration because of that mutual interest."

Earlier this year, it was revealed that Health and Human Services secretary Kathleen Sebelius may have sought to exploit this symbiotic relationship by illegally soliciting donations from insurance companies for Enroll America, a 501(c)(3) nonprofit group dedicated to maximizing Obamacare enrollment.

The law's disastrous rollout, however, is beginning to strain this tentative alliance. The president himself has thus far refrained from directly attacking the insurance industry, but the initial White House response to the uproar over mass policy cancellations—something Obama repeatedly pledged wouldn't happen to anyone—was to insist that Obamacare had nothing to do with it, implicitly faulting the insurance companies that canceled the policies (to comply with Obamacare).

Following the president's announcement on Thursday, the insurance industry fired back. "The only reason consumers are getting notices about their current coverage changing is because the ACA [Affordable Care Act] requires all policies to cover a broad range of benefits that go beyond what many people choose to purchase today," Karen Ignagni, president of America's Health Insurance Plans, said in a statement issued during the president's news conference. "Changing the rules after health plans have already met the requirements of the law could destabilize the market and result in higher premiums for consumers."

The industry is . . . facing more than $100 billion in new taxes . . . which will almost certainly cause premiums to rise even further, especially if enrollment in the exchanges remains low and consists largely of older, sicker individuals.

The Obama administration can hardly afford to further alienate the insurance industry. Its cooperation and participation in the exchanges is required if the law has any chance of success. At the same time, insurance companies need a fully functioning exchange so that people can actually enroll in and pay for policies.

Some state insurance regulators have already refused to play along with Obama's latest "fix," the legality of which is questionable at best, and will not allow insurance companies to continue to offer health plans that were canceled for noncompliance. Congress may well provide a more formal and expansive fix to the problem, but there remain a host of pressing issues that are likely to further test the industry's relationship with the White House.

Insurance companies are already lobbying furiously to reduce the impact of nearly $200 billion worth of cuts to Medicare Advantage, the system of privately administered Medicare plans approved by the federal government. After being delayed until after the 2012 election, the cuts are scheduled to go into effect next year. The industry is also facing more than $100 billion in new taxes on insurance plans beginning next year, which will almost certainly cause premiums to rise even further, especially if enrollment in the exchanges remains low and consists largely of older, sicker individuals. The White House will no doubt be tempted to blame insurance companies for any significant increase in the price of health plans, regardless of the cause.

But even if the exchanges don't live up to expectations, insurance companies will receive a partial bailout for losses over the next three years, thanks to a little-noticed (but extensively lobbied for, no doubt) provision in the law that Senator Marco Rubio (R., Fla.) is now trying to repeal, after noting that the president's latest fix will only increase the likelihood of a taxpayer bailout.

A vote on Rubio's plan would put Democrats and the White House in the politically dicey situation of defending the insurance companies' right to a bailout, or of inciting their wrath in such a way that it could finally blow up a relationship crucial to Obamacare as we know it.

9

The Affordable Care Act Will Hurt the US Economy

Sara Marie Brenner

Sara Marie Brenner is the creator and editor of Brenner Brief.com and host of the conservative Brenner Brief *radio show.*

The Affordable Care Act (ACA) is a harmful piece of legislation that will negatively affect the US economy. First and foremost, the ACA will be bad for businesses and job creation because it will force employers to offer a minimum standard of health-care coverage for their employees. Because doing so will significantly raise the cost of doing business, employers will have no choice but to lay off employees or to reduce their hours so that they do not have to comply with the requirements of the ACA and can thereby protect company profits. The ACA is an absolute disaster for businesses, and Republicans need to figure out how to defund it before the act does further damage to the country's economy.

President Barack Obama attempted again today [September 26, 2013] to sell his signature legislation, Obamacare, just a few days before its launch. Given the poll numbers and recent stories, it appears even his messianic complex couldn't convince Americans that Obamacare is actually good for them. And, news stories over the last year demonstrate the intrinsic damage his law is having on this nation's economy.

The president said at Prince George's Community College in Maryland today, "I will not negotiate on anything when it comes to the full faith and credit of the United States of America."

It is grossly disingenuous to claim that the Republican attempt to defund or delay that trainwreck of a healthcare takeover jeopardizes America's credit rating.

If Obama will negotiate with Russia, Syria and Iran when it comes to the international security interests of this nation, he should at least make attempts for compromise with the majority party in the U.S. House.

Since Obama cannot be bothered to come to an agreement with the GOP [Republican party], the stories continue to mount demonstrating that Obamacare will be a heavy blow to small businesses, job creation and the economy. While Obama spoke to a college audience today about his excellent law, that same monstrosity was negatively impacting colleges all across the country.

Employees Cut Hours to Avoid ACA

In July, the *Tampa Tribune* reported that two of the premiere public colleges in the area would be cutting adjunct faculty members' hours to comply with Obamacare.

"The area's two premiere public colleges are among a growing number cutting the hours of adjunct faculty members to keep them from qualifying for coverage under the Affordable Care Act [ACA], President Barack Obama's initiative to get more Americans insured. Hillsborough Community College and St. Petersburg College officials say there's nothing insidious about the strategy—that instead, it's an economic necessity in an environment where elevating their largely part-time faculties to health-benefit status could cost millions of dollars they don't have."

In April, an AP [Associated Press] reporter shared a story about Virginia Community College professors who would see their hours cut. Again, this was due to Obamacare.

We all want to grow, we all want to offer our employees healthcare, but there's just not enough pots [of money] to do all of these things.

"Many adjunct instructors at Virginia's 23 community colleges will see their hours cut starting this summer thanks to Virginia's response to the new federal health reform law, a change that could cripple or kill livelihoods teachers like Ann Hubbard worked hard to build."

The *Pittsburgh Post-Gazette* reported in November, 2012, that 400 temporary part-time employees at the Community College of Pennsylvania's Allegheny County were told their hours would be cut. Once again, this is due to Obamacare.

"To Community College of Allegheny County's president, Alex Johnson, cutting hours for some 400 temporary part-time workers to avoid providing health insurance coverage for them under the impending Affordable Health Care Act is purely a cost-saving measure at a time the college faces a funding reduction."

In Ohio, WHIZ reported that a business is dropping health insurance for its employees because of Obamacare. Steve Gaswint, owner of Black Run Transmission, says, "Small businesses can't grow when they're unsure what their costs in the future will be, when they're unsure what their labor costs will be. We all want to grow, we all want to offer our employees healthcare, but there's just not enough pots to do all of these things."

Uncertainty for Small Businesses

Roger Geiger, a VP with the National Federation of Independent Business [NFIB] and Executive Director of NFIB Ohio, also comments in WHIZ's report, "Small business owners just don't know what to expect with all of the mandates, all of the new requirements. We think it's having a terrible effect on job creation. Business owners are not taking the risk in hiring people right now because of this."

Also in Ohio, the Cleveland Clinic announced last week that it would be cutting jobs and slashing five to six percent of its $6 billion annual budget, all to prepare for Obamacare. The Cleveland Clinic is the second largest employer in Ohio.

In a story for Reuters, Eileen Sheil, Executive Director of Corporate Communications for the Cleveland Clinic Foundation, explains. "Some of the initiatives include offering early retirement to 3,000 eligible employees, reducing operational costs, stricter review of filling vacant positions, and lastly workforce reductions." Furthermore, Bloomberg reports that "The move is designed to help the clinic and its patients prepare for the Affordable Care Act . . ."

Tuesday [September 24, 2013], the *Washington Examiner* quoted Florida Congresswoman Debbie Wasserman-Schultz, the head of the Democratic National Committee, who conceded, "we must not treat every minute provision in the law as sacred," and those supporting the law "should be open to suggestions for improving the law."

As a breast cancer survivor, Wasserman-Schultz has more experience with this nation's health care system than someone who has not suffered serious illness. Perhaps she is more likely to understand that it is imperative that the quality of care remain high for Americans seeking care.

All of this is happening amidst reports that the IRS [Internal Revenue Service] slush fund set aside to handle hiring, training and organizing in preparation for being the administrators of Obamacare regulations, is missing $67 million. In the scheme of things that may sound like a miniscule dollar amount, but the fact that the IRS cannot track its own money leaves us to wonder how they plan to account for the health-care status for every one of the 310 million residents in the United States.

As *The Washington Times* hypothesized Wednesday on the possibility that the House GOP could demand a delay in the individual mandate. Speaker [John] Boehner announced Thursday that the House intends to do just that. Breaking ranks with his Democrat colleagues, Sen. Joe Manchin, D-W.V., says of the proposal: "There's no way I could not vote for it. . . . It's very reasonable and sensible."

The Affordable Care Act Is a Disaster

Obamacare is not resulting in more people being insured, more people being cared for, lowered costs, keeping our doctors or plans, or anything else we were promised. What it is becoming, however, is the biggest bait and switch this country has ever seen.

As fewer people seek care due to rising out of pocket costs, and patients have their treatment delayed as they search for a new doctor because their current physician isn't in their plan, this atrocious law could bankrupt this nation and literally kill Americans.

Obamacare is nothing but a trainwreck, and Republicans must create an effective strategy to defund and prevent the law's full implementation.

10

The Affordable Care Act Should Be Repealed

The Heritage Foundation

The Heritage Foundation is a conservative think tank based in Washington, DC.

The Affordable Care Act (ACA) is bad for America. As such, it should be repealed, and the government should undertake a series of market-based, patient-centered reforms instead. Those reforms should be based on five principles: 1) choose, control, and carry your own health insurance; 2) let free markets provide the insurance and health-care services that people want; 3) encourage employers to provide a portable health insurance benefit to employees; 4) assist those who need help through civil society, the free market, and the states; and 5) protect the right of conscience and unborn children. The ACA moves the country in the wrong direction, and Congress should repeal the law in its entirety. Patient-centered, market-based reform would be a much more effective way to improve the American health-care system.

To allow Americans to reclaim control of their own health care and benefit from competition in a free market for insurance and health care, Congress should repeal the Obamacare statute and enact patient-centered, market-based reforms based on five principles:

- Choose, control, and carry your own health insurance;

- Let free markets provide the insurance and health care services that people want;

- Encourage employers to provide a portable health insurance benefit to employees;

- Assist those who need help through civil society, the free market, and the states; and

- Protect the right of conscience and unborn children.

The Patient Protection and Affordable Care Act (Obamacare) moves health care in the wrong direction. It puts government, not patients, in charge of individual health care decisions. Moreover, it fails to meet the promises laid out by President Barack Obama. With each passing day, it becomes clearer that Obamacare will not reduce premiums for average American families, bend the cost curve in health care spending, or bring down the deficit. For these reasons, among others, Obamacare must be repealed.

Rather than following Obamacare's example of forcing Americans into government-run health insurance exchanges, true patient-centered reform of health care would make insurance more portable.

However, a return to the status quo before Obamacare is not the final step. Policymakers should pursue reforms based on five basic principles. Adopting such reforms would move American health care in the right direction: toward a patient-centered, market-based health care system.

Principle #1: Choose, Control, and Carry Your Own Health Insurance

True health reform should promote personal ownership of health insurance. While Obamacare uses government-run insurance exchanges to limit individual choice, real reforms would focus on encouraging Americans to purchase insurance policies that they can take with them from job to job and into retirement in a competitive, free market. Policymakers should enact several key changes for this culture of personal health care ownership to take root.

Portability. Most Americans obtain coverage through their place of work. This allows employers to provide tax-free health benefits to their employees, while individuals purchasing health insurance on their own must use after-tax dollars. As a result, most individuals with private health insurance obtain that coverage from their employer.

Rather than following Obamacare's example of forcing Americans into government-run health insurance exchanges, true patient-centered reform of health care would make insurance more portable. Individuals should be able to purchase an insurance policy when they are young and carry that policy with them throughout their working lives into retirement.

Equal Tax Relief. While Obamacare alters the tax treatment of health insurance, it does so in a way that increases burdens on taxpayers. Its 40 percent tax on so-called Cadillac health insurance plans is but one of 18 separate tax increases included in the law, which, according to the Congressional Budget Office and the Joint Committee on Taxation, will raise $771 billion in revenue from 2013 to 2022.

A better approach would equalize the tax treatment of health insurance *without* raising new revenues. The Heritage Foundation has previously proposed replacing the existing deduction for employer-provided health coverage with a flat tax credit that individuals could use to purchase a health insurance policy of their own. Another idea, first proposed by then-President George W. Bush, would give all Americans purchasing health coverage—whether through an employer or on their own—the same standard deduction for health insurance.

Both proposals assume revenue neutrality over ten years. Unlike Obamacare, they do not propose using reform to increase net tax revenues.

Both of these proposals would accomplish two important objectives.

Tax Incentives

First, they would equalize the tax treatment between health coverage provided through an employer and health coverage purchased by an individual. Providing equal tax treatment would remove a major obstacle that discourages individuals from buying and holding their own health insurance policy for years and taking that coverage from job to job. Tax equity would also encourage firms either to provide direct contributions toward their workers' health coverage or to increase wages in place of health benefits.

The most important element of any health care system is the trusted relationship between doctor and patient.

Second, limiting the amount of the tax benefit provided, either with a tax credit or with a standard deduction, would encourage individuals to become smarter purchasers of health insurance coverage. Studies have demonstrated that the current uncapped tax benefit for employer-provided health insurance encourages firms to offer richer health plans and individuals to overconsume health care. According to the Congressional Budget Office, reforming the tax treatment of health insurance "would provide stronger incentives for enrollees to weigh the expected benefits and costs of policies" when buying insurance, thus helping to reduce costs.

Choice of Providers. Through its new system of government control, Obamacare restricts choice and access for many patients. The nonpartisan Medicare actuary concluded that the Medicare reimbursement reductions in Obamacare could make 40 percent of all hospitals unprofitable in the long term, thus restricting beneficiary access to care. Moreover, preliminary reports suggest that Obamacare's insurance exchanges will feature limited provider networks in an attempt to mitigate premium increases for individuals purchasing exchange coverage.

The most important element of any health care system is the trusted relationship between doctor and patient. Any system of truly patient-centered health care should work to preserve those important bonds and to repair the damage to those bonds caused by Obamacare.

Encouraging Personal Savings. Since their creation in 2004, health savings accounts (HSAs) have become a popular way for millions of families to build savings for needed health care expenses. HSA plans combine a health insurance option featuring a slightly higher deductible—but catastrophic protection in the event of significant medical expenses—with a tax-free savings account. As one of several new consumer-driven health options, HSAs encourage patients to take control of their own health care, providing financial incentives for consumers to serve as wise health care purchasers.

Over the past several years, millions of families have taken advantage of the innovative tools that HSA plans offer. The number of people enrolled in HSA-eligible policies has skyrocketed from 1 million in March 2005 to 15.5 million in January 2013. Numerous studies have also shown that individuals with HSA plans have used tools provided by their health insurer to become more involved with their health care—for example, by using online support tools, inquiring about provider cost and quality, and seeking preventive care. As a result, individuals had saved at least $12.4 billion in their HSAs by the end of 2011.

However, HSA holders still face obstacles to building their personal savings. For instance, under current law, funds contributed to an HSA may not be used to pay for insurance premiums, except under very limited circumstances. Changing this restriction and increasing HSA contribution limits would enhance both personal savings and personal ownership of health insurance.

Coverage for Pre-Existing Conditions

The problem of providing access to individuals with pre-existing conditions, while very real, did not necessitate the massive changes in America's health care system included in Obamacare. In 2011, the Obama Administration suggested that as many as 129 million Americans with pre-existing conditions were "at risk" and "could be denied coverage" without Obamacare's massive changes in America's insurance markets.

State insurance markets suffer from two flaws: Many markets are uncompetitive ... and costly benefit mandates raise health insurance premiums.

That claim was wildly untrue. Under prior law, individuals with employer-sponsored coverage (90 percent of the private market) could not be subjected to pre-existing condition exclusions. In fact, prior to Obamacare, the number of individuals with pre-existing conditions who truly could not obtain health coverage was vastly smaller, and the problem existed only in the individual market. It is therefore not surprising that, according to the most recent data, only an estimated 134,708 individuals have enrolled in the supplemental federal high-risk pool program since it was created under Obamacare to, cover individuals with pre-existing conditions—still less than the 200,000 individuals originally projected to enroll.

States could use a variety of approaches to provide coverage to individuals who are unable to purchase insurance. For instance, 35 states already operate high-risk pools with a collective current enrollment of 227,000 individuals to ensure access to coverage for individuals with pre-existing conditions.

Alternatively, states could establish reinsurance or risk transfer mechanisms under which insurance companies would reimburse each other for the cost of treating individuals with high medical expenses without added funding from state or federal taxpayers. Either approach would be far preferable to the massive amounts of regulation, taxation, and government spending under Obamacare.

Principle #2: Let Free Markets Provide the Insurance and Health Care Services That People Want

Many individuals have already learned that, due in part to Obamacare, with its government-run health exchanges, new bureaucracies, and other forms of government control, they will not be able to retain their current health insurance. There is a better way, and it involves providing more choice through market incentives rather than undermining markets through centralized bureaucracy.

Cross-State Purchasing. Currently, state insurance markets suffer from two flaws: Many markets are uncompetitive, with up to 70 percent of metropolitan areas considered "highly concentrated," and costly benefit mandates raise health insurance premiums. A prior Heritage Foundation analysis found that each benefit mandate raises costs by an average of approximately $0.75 per month. Another study found that states have imposed a total of 2.271 benefit mandates—or approximately 45 per state. Taken together, these two studies suggest that the cumulative effect of these mandates could raise premiums by $20–$40 per month, or hundreds of dollars per year.

Congress can help to mitigate these problems by removing federal barriers to interstate commerce in health insurance products. Individuals should have the ability to purchase insurance products across state lines, choosing the health plan that best meets their needs regardless of the location of its issuer.

Pooling Mechanisms. Another way to improve patient choice and make insurance markets more competitive would involve new purchasing arrangements and pooling mechanisms. Small businesses, individual membership associations, religious groups, and fraternal organizations should be able to sell health insurance policies through new group purchasing arrangements. The federal government's role should be to remove the barriers to such arrangements.

The Medicare reimbursement reductions in Obamacare will make 15 percent of all hospitals unprofitable within the decade and 40 percent unprofitable by 2050.

By extending the benefits of group coverage beyond the place of work, these new purchasing arrangements would also encourage portability of health insurance coverage. These reforms would allow individuals to obtain their health plan from a trusted source—one with which they would be likely to have a longer association than they have with their employer—thereby creating a form of health coverage that Americans could truly own.

Reforming Medicare

Seniors could also benefit from patient-centered Medicare reforms, one of which should help to restore the doctor-patient relationship. Congress should eliminate the anticompetitive restrictions that prevent doctors and patients from contracting privately for medical services outside of traditional Medicare. Congress can also restructure the Medicare benefit, modernizing the design of a program that has remained largely unchanged since its creation nearly 50 years ago. These changes would enhance patient choice while preserving the program's solvency for future generations of Americans.

Regrettably, Obamacare imposes many its most harmful effects on senior citizens. According to the Medicare actuary, the Medicare reimbursement reductions in Obamacare will make 15 percent of all hospitals unprofitable within the decade and 40 percent unprofitable by 2050. As a result, seniors may face significant obstacles to obtaining health care in the future.

There is a better way. Specifically, Congress should provide seniors with a generous subsidy to purchase a Medicare plan of their choosing. Seniors who choose a plan costing less than the subsidy would pay less, while seniors who choose a plan costing more than the subsidy would pay the difference in price.

Consumer Choice and Competition. As part of its system of government control, Obamacare hinders patients' ability to choose their own health plan. One survey found that the mandates and requirements in the law mean that more than half of all insurance policies purchased directly by individuals will not qualify as "government-approved" under Obamacare. As a result, many Americans are finding that they will not be able to keep the health plan they have and like—despite President Obama's repeated promises.

Moving to a defined contribution model for health insurance would allow workers to buy a health insurance policy in their youth and take that policy with them from job to job into retirement.

True patient-centered reform would bolster HSAs and other consumer-directed health products—such as health reimbursement arrangements and flexible spending accounts—that have the ability to transform American health care. One study published in the prestigious journal *Health Affairs* in 2012 found that expanding market penetration of consumer-driven health plans from 13 percent to 50 percent of all employers could reduce health costs by as much as $73.6 billion per year—a reduction in health spending of 9.1 percent.

In other words, expanding consumer choice and competition could *reduce* health care costs and spending—the opposite of Obamacare, which restricts consumer choice and *increases* health costs and spending.

Principle #3: Encourage Employers to Provide a Portable Health Insurance Benefit

Because most Americans traditionally have received health insurance from their employers, many individuals have few, if any, choices when selecting a health plan. According to the broadest survey of employer plans, nearly nine in 10 firms (87 percent) offer only one plan type, and only 2 percent offer three or more plan types. As a result, employees have only a very limited ability to choose the plan that best meets their needs.

Defined Contribution. An ideal solution would convert the traditional system of employer-provided health insurance from a defined benefit model to a defined contribution model. Rather than providing health insurance directly, employers instead would offer cash contributions to their workers, enabling them to buy the plans of their own choosing. Combined with changes in the tax treatment of health insurance and regulatory improvements to enhance portability, moving to a defined contribution model for health insurance would allow workers to buy a health insurance policy in their youth and take that policy with them from job to job into retirement. These changes would also enable workers and families to negotiate contributions from multiple employers rather than having just one employer foot the bill.

Principle #4: Assist Those Who Need Help Through Civil Society, the Free Market, and States

While some health reforms—such as changing the tax treatment of health insurance and reforming the Medicare program—remain fully within the purview of the federal government, states also play a critical role in enacting reforms that can lower costs, improve access to care, and modernize state Medicaid programs. By serving as the "laboratories of democracy," states can provide examples for other states—and the federal government—to follow. Because many state-based reforms do not rely on Washington's involvement or approval, states can move ahead with innovative market-based solutions even as federal bureaucrats attempt to implement Obamacare's government-centric approach.

Obamacare makes Medicaid's problems worse, consigning millions more Americans to this poor government-run program.

State Innovation. If given proper time and space by an all-too-intrusive federal government, states can act on their own to open their insurance markets. A few states have already acted to open their insurance markets. In 2011, Georgia enacted legislation allowing interstate purchasing of health insurance, and Maine passed legislation allowing carriers from other New England states to offer insurance products to its citizens. Just before Obamacare was enacted in 2010, Wyoming acted to permit out-of-state insurers to offer products. While it may take some time before a critical mass of states creates a true interstate market for insurance, these nascent efforts demonstrate the nationwide interest in expanding health insurance choice and competition.

Medicaid Premium Assistance. Among various forms of health coverage, the Medicaid program is known for its poor quality and outcomes for patients. Numerous studies have found that Medicaid patients suffer worse outcomes than other patients suffer. A recent study from Oregon concluded that after two years, patients in Medicaid did not achieve measurable health benefits from their insurance coverage. Even participants—recognizing that many physicians, because of the program's low reimbursement rates, will not treat Medicaid patients—complain that the program is not "real insurance."

Obamacare makes Medicaid's problems worse, consigning millions more Americans to this poor government-run program. True reform would instead subsidize private health insurance for low-income Medicaid beneficiaries. The Heritage Foundation has previously promoted such a solution as part of its comprehensive reform of the Medicaid program. Congress should take steps to encourage states to provide premium assistance. Such programs would promote health care ownership and provide beneficiaries with better access to care than the traditional Medicaid program does.

The Congressional Budget Office concluded that enacting comprehensive liability reform would reduce health care spending by tens of billions of dollars per year.

Reforming Medicaid

Despite the looming presence of Obamacare, states should continue wherever possible to seek opportunities to reform their Medicaid programs, moving toward more personalized care and including strong incentives for personal responsibility. States can also seek additional flexibility from Washington to modernize care; many governors have already made such requests.

Congress also should act to reform and modernize Medicaid. Efforts in this vein would include comprehensive reforms—such as a block grant or per capita spending caps—that trade additional flexibility for states in exchange for a fixed spending allotment from Washington. Other reforms could incentivize and subsidize Medicaid beneficiaries to move to private insurance policies that they can own and keep. All of these reforms would focus on modernizing Medicaid to provide better quality care, reduce costs, and promote personal responsibility and ownership.

Reducing Fraud. Regrettably, many government health programs are riddled with fraud. Some estimates suggest that as much as $60 billion in Medicare spending may involve fraud. Similar problems plague many state Medicaid programs. A 2005 *New York Times* exposé on Medicaid fraud quoted James Mehmet, a former chief investigator in New York State, as saying that 10 percent of the state's Medicaid spending constituted outright fraud, with another 20 percent to 30 percent comprising "unnecessary spending that might not be criminal." Overall, Mehmet estimated that "questionable" Medicaid spending totaled $18 billion in New York State alone.

Congress and the states should do more to crack down on the waste, fraud, and abuse that plague America's health entitlements. Reforms should end the current "pay and chase" model, under which investigators must attempt to track down fraudulent claims and providers after they have already received reimbursement. Other solutions would enhance penalties for those who engage in fraudulent activity—for instance, buying or selling personal patient information, which is often used to perpetrate fraud schemes. These and other reforms would save taxpayer dollars, helping to preserve Medicare and Medicaid for future generations.

Removing Barriers to Care

With studies indicating that America faces a doctor shortage in future years, policymakers should focus on removing barriers that discourage institutions from assisting those who need health care. Regrettably, America's litigious culture has resulted in the widespread practice of defensive medicine by doctors and other health practitioners. In response, some states have changed their medical liability laws to discourage frivolous lawsuits, prompting doctors to move to those states to practice medicine. Were other states to adopt such reforms, this would encourage doctors—a majority of whom believe the practice of medicine is in jeopardy—to remain in practice and would encourage students to join the profession.

In addition, reforms that improve the liability system could reduce the prevalence of defensive medicine practices and thereby help to reduce health costs. One government estimate found that reasonable limits on non-economic damages could reduce total health spending by as much as $126 billion per year by reducing the amount of defensive medicine practiced by physicians. More recently, the Congressional Budget Office concluded that enacting comprehensive liability reform would reduce health care spending by tens of billions of dollars per year, reducing the federal budget deficit by tens of billions over the next decade.

Regrettably, Obamacare ... [forces] many employers to offer, and individuals to purchase, health coverage that violates the core tenets of their faith regarding the protection of life.

To help to eliminate barriers to care and reduce health costs, states should reform their liability systems, capping non-economic damages and taking other steps to reduce the incidence of frivolous lawsuits and ensure proper legal protections for health care providers. However, because liability reform and torts in general are properly a state issue, Congress should not impose liability reforms except where the federal government has a clear, constitutionally based federal interest. Examples might include liability reforms with respect to medical products approved by the federal Food and Drug Administration or when the federal government is a payer of health care services, as it is with Medicare and Medicaid.

Reforming Scope-of-Practice and Certificate of Need. State governments control the licensure of both medical professionals and medical practices. By removing artificial obstacles that restrict the supply of medical providers, states can expand access to health services across populations while unleashing new competition that can work to reduce costs.

States can reform their health care systems by reexamining scope-of-practice laws, which frequently limit the ability of nurse practitioners and other health professionals to care for patients. In 2010, the Institute of Medicine concluded that "state regulations often restrict the ability of nurses to provide care legally" and that policymakers should remove "barriers that limit the ability of nurses to practice to the full extent of their education, training, and competence." Many states have begun to reform their scope-of-practice laws to allow physician assistants, nurse practitioners, and others to treat more patients even as entrenched interests have fought to preserve their preferential treatment. States should follow the recommendations of the Institute of Medicine in reforming their scope-of-practice laws to allow all medical professionals to practice to the full extent of their training.

A total of 36 states also impose certificate-of-need requirements, which impede the introduction of new hospitals and medical facilities. These laws require organizations seeking to build new medical facilities to obtain a certificate from a state board that the facility is "needed" in a particular area. As with scope-of-practice requirements, reforming or eliminating certificate-of-need restrictions would encourage the development of new medical facilities, expanding access to care and giving patients more choices.

Principle #5: Protect the Right of Conscience and Unborn Children

Government should not compel individuals to undertake actions that violate their deeply held religious beliefs. Regrettably, Obamacare imposes just such a requirement on Americans, forcing many employers to offer, and individuals to purchase, health coverage that violates the core tenets of their faith regarding the protection of life.

Congress should ensure that individuals never again are required to violate their religious beliefs to meet a government diktat.

Rights of Conscience. Congress should protect the rights of consumers, insurers, employers, and medical personnel to refrain from facilitating, participating in, funding, or providing services contrary to their consciences or the tenets of their religious faith. Enacting these protections would prevent Americans from facing the moral dilemma presented by Obamacare, which has forced individuals, employers, and religious organizations to choose between violating the law and violating their faith or consciences.

Permanent Prohibition on Taxpayer-Funded Abortion. Congress should make permanent in law the existing annually enacted prohibitions on the use of federal taxpayer funds to finance abortions or health insurance coverage that includes elective abortions. These protections, enacted as the "Hyde Amendment" every year since 1976, prevent the use of taxpayer dollars to fund elective abortions. After nearly 40 years of renewing these protections on an annual basis, Congress should finally make them permanent in law.

A New Vision for Health Reform

Obamacare moves American health care in the wrong direction. Not only does the law raise health costs rather than lowering them, but it creates new bureaucracies that will erode the doctor–patient relationship. The trillions of dollars in new spending for Obamacare will place a massive fiscal burden on future generations of taxpayers. For these reasons and more, Congress should repeal the law in its entirety.

Once this has been done, policymakers should then advance health reforms that move toward patient-centered, market-based health care. Such reforms would promote personal choice and ownership of health insurance: enable the free market to respond to consumer demands; encourage portability of coverage for workers; help civil society, the free markets, and the states to assist those in need; and protect the rights of faith, conscience, and life.

11

Most Americans Oppose Repealing the Affordable Care Act

Ronald Brownstein

Ronald Brownstein is the editorial director for Atlantic Media. He writes a weekly column for National Journal *and regularly contributes other articles for the* Journal, Quartz, *and* The Atlantic *magazines.*

*Even though it got off to a rocky start in the public eye, most Americans oppose repealing the Affordable Care Act (ACA), and their opinions about the law have not changed much since the summer before it was enacted. According to a recent poll by United Technologies/*National Journal *Congressional Connection, only 35 percent of those surveyed said the law should be repealed—roughly the same number who answered the same way six months before the law went into effect. As expected, the poll showed a clear split between Republicans and Democrats on the issue. A majority of Democrats say they expect the law to ultimately improve the US health-care system, while nine out of ten self-identified Republicans called the law "fatally flawed."*

Despite sharp divisions over the long-term impact of President [Barack] Obama's health-reform law [the Affordable Care Act (ACA)] fewer than two in five Americans say it should be repealed, virtually unchanged since last summer [2013], the latest United Technologies/*National Journal* Congressional Connection Poll has found.

Amid all the tumult over the law's troubled implementation, the survey found that public opinion about it largely follows familiar political tracks and has changed remarkably little since the summer on the critical question of what Congress should do next. On that measure, support for repeal has not significantly increased among any major group except Republicans and working-class whites since the Congressional Connection Poll last tested opinion on the question in July.

While the survey found a slim majority believes the law will do more to hurt than help the nation's health care system over time, it also found the statute retains majority support among key elements of the modern Democratic coalition, including minorities, college-educated white women, and young people. That means Congressional Democrats inclined to distance themselves from the law in the hope of placating skeptical independent or Republican-leaning voters face the risk of alienating some of their core supporters.

Republicans Still Don't Like the ACA

Conversely, the overwhelming opposition to the law within the GOP [Republican] coalition—with nearly nine in ten self-identified Republicans calling the law "fundamentally flawed" and nearly three-fourths of them supporting its repeal—ensures that Republican legislators will continue to face grassroots pressure to roll it back, by any means available.

On the broadest question of the law's ultimate impact, the survey found adults tilting narrowly toward skepticism. The survey asked respondents, considering "everything happening with the implementation of the federal health care law" to choose between two statements about its eventual effect. A slim 52 percent majority agreed with the negative assessment: "The law is fundamentally flawed and will do more to hurt the nation's health care system than improve it." Another 46 percent endorsed the more positive sentiment: "The law is experiencing temporary problems and will ultimately produce a better health care system for the country."

Opinions on this fundamental choice divided the country in patterns recognizable from the last several elections. Most dramatically, almost exactly three-fifths of whites (59 percent) described the law as fundamentally flawed, while just over three-fifths of minorities (62 percent) said it will ultimately improve the health care system.

Opinions from other core elements of each party's base lined up predictably, as well. Opposition spiked among the cornerstones of the GOP coalition: the share who described the law as fundamentally flawed reached 65 percent of whites without a college education (including 70 percent of such noncollege-educated white men); 64 percent among rural residents; 58 percent among whites older than 50; and 54 percent among respondents from the South.

Thirty-eight percent of those polled said Congress should "repeal the law so it is not implemented at all," while 35 percent said lawmakers should "wait and see how things go before making any changes."

Democrats Remain Supportive of the ACA

By contrast, the groups central to the Democratic electoral coalition, generally remained supportive of the law, although by narrower margins. Along with the roughly three-fifths of minorities, 52 percent of adults younger than 30, and 55 percent of college-educated white women say the law will ultimately improve the health care system. College-educated white men are often a difficult group for Democrats, but a thin 51 percent majority of them also said the law will ultimately produce improvements.

Though in most respects following familiar lines, these results do contain some clear warning signs for Democrats. One is that the support level for the law among minorities has dipped well below the four-fifths of their votes Obama attracted in 2012. Another is that the law faces skepticism from independents, with 55 percent saying it is fundamentally flawed and only 42 percent maintaining that it will eventually improve the health care system. Just 36 percent of white independents expect the law to generate net benefits; 61 percent said they consider it fundamentally flawed.

Yet the survey did not find these doubts about the law translating into surging demand to undo it. Reprising a question first asked in July, the survey recorded a close split when respondents were asked to choose among three options for what Congress "should do now about the health care law."

Thirty-eight percent of those polled said Congress should "repeal the law so it is not implemented at all," while 35 percent said lawmakers should "wait and see how things go before making any changes." Another 23 percent said Congress should "provide more money to ensure it is implemented effectively" (the remaining 5 percent had no opinion).

Few Changes Since Last Poll

Notwithstanding all the tumult surrounding the law's rocky implementation, those numbers changed little from July, when 36 percent supported repeal, 30 percent wanted Congress to wait and see, and 27 percent wanted lawmakers to provide more funds for implementation.

Just like the question of the law's ultimate impact, this choice divided the country along familiar lines. What's more, the new results showed striking-stability since last July for almost all major subgroups.

Since last July's poll, support for repeal has oscillated only slightly (or not at all) for self-identified Democrats (9 percent now, unchanged since July) and independents (40 percent now compared with 41 percent then); whites (48 percent versus 44 percent) and nonwhites (unchanged at 16 percent); young adults under 30 (unchanged at 26 percent) and seniors (42 percent now versus 40 percent then). The survey recorded a somewhat bigger shift toward repeal among whites without a college degree (up to 53 percent from 46 percent last summer) and self-identified Republicans (74 percent now, from 65 percent last summer). But whites with at least a four-year college degree remained essentially unchanged, with 36 percent now backing repeal, compared with 39 percent in July. The United Technologies/*National Journal* Congressional Connection Poll, conducted by Princeton Survey Research Associates International, surveyed 1,013 adults by landline and cell phone from Nov. 14–17, 2013. It has a margin of error of plus or minus 3.6 percentage points.

Indeed, like the question over the law's eventual impact, this measure found clear signs of doubt among the key elements of the modern Democratic coalition, but no indication that they are rushing to abandon health reform: Repeal drew support from just one-sixth of minorities, one-fourth of millennials, and one-third of college-educated white women, the groups on which Democrats now rely most.

12

Calling the Affordable Care Act "Obamacare" Undermines Reform

Mugambi Jouet

Mugambi Jouet is a French writer, scholar, and human rights lawyer who writes about American exceptionalism and politics for media outlets such as Salon, Huffington Post, *and* Collier's Magazine.

When critics of the Affordable Care Act (ACA) first referred to the law as "Obamacare," it was meant as a derogatory term. Since then, President Barack Obama himself has adopted the nickname to refer to his signature health-care reform program. Looking back, it was not a good idea for him to do so. Calling the ACA "Obamacare" undermines the health-care reform effort in several ways: 1) it ties the popularity of the law to the president's popularity; 2) it implies that the ACA is an Obama pet project; 3) it suggests that health-care-for-all is an Obama or liberal idea; 4) it suggests that health-care reform is not a serious policy matter; and 5) the term arose as part of a disinformation campaign. The ACA should not be called "Obamacare," especially by its supporters.

"Obamacare" was initially perceived as a derogatory term advanced by opponents of health care reform. Yet, the term is now commonly used by both conservatives and liberals as a way to refer to the Patient Protection and Affordable

Care Act. As the government shutdown crisis unfolded, politicians, the media, and ordinary citizens debated the pros and cons of "Obamacare." The shutdown is now over, and it is widely reported that congressional Republicans failed to repeal, defund or postpone "Obamacare." The legislation may stay the same but its derogatory label has stuck.

The change in attitude partly comes from President [Barack] Obama, who has sought to coopt criticism of the Affordable Care Act by embracing the term "Obamacare." In 2011, Obama even said "That's right—I care," in an attempt to dismiss those who have vilified "Obamacare." In retrospect, this seems like a dubious strategy. While the label "Obamacare" is not negative per se, there are multiple reasons why it undermines health care reform.

Why "Obamacare" Undermines Reform

1) The word "Obamacare" ties the law's popularity to Obama's popularity: Indeed, if you are not an Obama supporter, how could you be for "Obamacare"? By definition, "Obamacare" cannot be popular insofar as Obama himself is relatively unpopular. Besides, tying the name of a major legislative reform to the name of a politician is questionable. Should Medicare be called "Johnsoncare" because it was passed under President Lyndon Johnson?

> *Using a frivolous term like "Obamacare" obscures the serious need for reform in a country where scores of ill people have been denied medical treatment or ruined by medical bills.*

2) "Obamacare" implies that the Affordable Care Act is an Obama pet project: While Obama has embraced this legislation as a politically-feasible reform, he hardly came up with it. In fact, the Affordable Care Act is modeled on past Republican proposals for a market-friendly reform that would hardly dismantle the current health insurance system. America is essentially the only Western democracy where insurance companies can profit from basic health care coverage.

3) "Obamacare" suggests that health-care-for-all is an Obama idea or a liberal idea: In reality, all developed countries except America have long had universal health care systems that go much further than the Affordable Care Act. All leading right-wing parties in Europe, Canada, Australia, New Zealand, and Japan have supported universal health care for decades. The vast majority of conservatives in other democratic countries do not consider universal health care a "liberal" policy.

4) "Obamacare" suggests that health care reform is not a serious policy matter: The label "Obamacare" was partly intended to mock the Affordable Care Act. Yet, the vast majority of health care law and policy experts worldwide agree that a form of universal health care is the best policy. Using a frivolous term like "Obamacare" obscures the serious need for reform in a country where scores of ill people have been denied medical treatment or ruined by medical bills.

5) The term "Obamacare" arose as part of a disinformation campaign: Labeling the law as "Obamacare" is a key part of the strategy of opponents of health care reform. This strategy has also entailed fear-mongering by using other misleading catch-words like "socialized medicine," "death panels," and a "government takeover of health care." It has likewise entailed misrepresenting basic facts. For instance, John Boehner claimed that "Obamacare" will wreck the "best" health care system worldwide—a blinkered view considering that 75 million Americans were either uninsured or critically underinsured before reform. By contrast, all other developed countries manage to provide universal health care with generally better or equal health results than America, which still has by far the highest overall health care costs worldwide.

Misleading Monikers

In sum, the Affordable Care Act should not be called "Obamacare," especially by its supporters. The fact that the media and much of the American public have accepted this derogatory term exemplifies the success of hard-line Republicans in framing the terms of the political debate. By the same token, referring to Medicare, Medicaid, and Social Security as "entitlements"—a term largely promoted by opponents of these programs—is misleading.

However, certain state governments are currently trying to implement the heath care law by avoiding self-defeating references to "Obamacare." Kentucky, will notably implement health care reform under the name "Kynect" while Idaho's program is named "Your Health Idaho." This pragmatic approach makes more sense than referring to reform as "Obamacare."

The Affordable Care Act has so far survived a shutdown crisis, a Supreme Court challenge, and two elections. Unless it is eventually repealed, it will shape American society for decades. This law is not fundamentally about Barack Obama but about much broader issues, which is another reason not to call it "Obamacare."

13

Misallocation of Obamacare Showcases Modern Race Bias

The Gazette

The Gazette *is a daily newspaper serving Colorado Springs and the Pikes Peak region of Colorado.*

Claiming that the term "Obamacare" is racist or otherwise insulting to President Barack Obama or to the Affordable Care Act is patently ridiculous. The name Obamacare caught on because it is short and catchy and much easier to say, and it fit in a sound bite or headline better than the clunky bureaucratic title of "Patient Protection and Affordable Care Act." Many laws are named after those who inspired or instigated them, and it is typically perceived as an honor that this is so; Obamacare should be no different. Additionally, to say that the moniker Obamacare is somehow derogatory because Obama is a black man is to suggest that Obama cannot handle the criticism typically bestowed on presidents. That in turn suggests that a black man can't handle it, which is its own special kind of racism.

Those who wonder if American racism has gone the way of dinosaurs should consider last week's misallocation of the term "Obamacare."

President Barack Obama managed to become the first black president in history. He's the first politician since 1956 to win at least 51 percent of the popular vote twice. By some accounts, he's the most powerful man in the world. As one man, he composes an entire branch of the federal government.

The president appears strong, intelligent, articulate and willing to take on challenges few others attempt. When he passed a law to overhaul the health care system—an accomplishment that would restructure one-sixth of the nation's economy—he did what no predecessor could, for better or worse.

Admire or dislike this president, he deserves credit for courage and rare ability to achieve political ends. Though he's often wrong, he exudes strength.

Yet, much of society does not treat him like a strong, capable man. Instead, they treat him as someone in need of dispensation from political tradition.

From Robert Redford to Oprah Winfrey to Chris Matthews to Harvey Weinstein—mentioning only a few recent examples—ardent supporters of Obama characterize his critics as "racist." They act as if past presidents enjoyed immunity from vitriolic opposition. Never mind the fact congressional opponents impeached two presidents and removed one from office. Forget that opponents of George W. Bush looked unceasingly for opportunities to impeach him and openly celebrated a movie that fantasized about his assassination. Forget all that, because presidential scrutiny was invented in 2008 by racists.

In truth, "Obamacare" caught on because the bureaucratic title "Patient Protection and Affordable Care Act" is boring, hard to say, even harder to remember and doesn't fit headline slots.

To suggest a man of Obama's intellect and achievement cannot handle intense criticism, traditionally meted out to presidents, is to say a black man can't handle it. To his credit,

Obama doesn't play the race card to counter even his most ardent critics—a fraction of whom may truly harbor racist motives.

The race-card defense of Obama reached a new level of absurdity this week when MSNBC host Melissa Harris-Perry referred to the term "Obamacare" as a concoction of "wealthy white men who needed a way to put themselves above and apart from a black man. To render him inferior and unequal and to diminish his accomplishments."

The journalist's accusation can be taken as a prejudiced assumption about evil "white men" she can't even identify by name. In truth, "Obamacare" caught on because the bureaucratic title "Patient Protection and Affordable Care Act" is boring, hard to say, even harder to remember and doesn't fit headline slots. "Obamacare" provides a friendly, catchy, more marketable way to speak of the law. It came about when Obama's approval ratings were near record highs, so the name "Obama" was far from derogatory.

Throughout history, we have named laws—along with cities, states, monuments, buildings and schools—after politicians. When then-first lady Hillary Rodham Clinton tried to overhaul health care, the media and public immediately coined "Hillarycare"—more than a decade before most Americans had heard of Barack Obama. When then-Gov. Mitt Romney, R-Mass., initiated state insurance reform, the law was dubbed "Romneycare." A bill to create Colorado's health care exchange was called "Amycare" because State Rep. Amy Stephens, a Monument Republican, introduced it. Supporters and opponents used it. We have Jessica's Law, Dodd-Frank, McCain-Feingold, Kristen's Law, Donna West Law, the Brady Act, Ryan White Care Act, the Lindbergh Law and the Bush Tax Cuts. The list of laws named for men, women, children and politicians who inspired them is long and distinguished.

"Obamacare" is neither positive nor negative. If the law somehow becomes a whopping success, the moniker will rightly honor a man who inspired it. If it continues to flop, the name will allocate blame. That's just politics, not a smoke-filled room of racist white men.

Barack Obama deserves respect for becoming the first black president, not insulting attempts to shield him from treatment that has long been part of political life. To act as if he is politically delicate, because he's black, just might be racist.

14

Botched ACA Rollout Could Taint President Obama's Legacy

Cleveland Plain Dealer

The Cleveland Plain Dealer *is a daily newspaper in Cleveland, Ohio.*

President Barack Obama's handling of the disastrous rollout of his signature health-care reform legislation—the Affordable Care Act (ACA)—was an even bigger debacle than the botched rollout itself. He handled the situation poorly, and in doing so eroded whatever confidence the public had in him and his health-care reform effort. Instead of simply reassuring people that things were going to get better soon, he should have rolled up his sleeves and gone to work to make sure that they actually did. He appeared to be out-of-touch and disconnected from the whole process, and his response to the ACA enrollment website problems did not inspire the public's confidence. President Obama needs to rededicate himself to the success of the ACA before it undermines his presidential legacy.

Instead of being remembered for fundamentally changing the health care landscape in America for the better, President Barack Obama may instead go down as one of the most disconnected, too-cool-for-school chief executives in U.S. history.

And he better hope that it doesn't get any worse than that, for his flubbing of the Obamacare rollout threatens the very success of what is otherwise a noble attempt to make sure everybody has adequate and affordable medical insurance.

That was the whole point of the Affordable Care Act when Obama signed it into law in 2010. And from that point on, despite the law's flaws, he should have made its execution his number one domestic priority. Obviously, he didn't.

Instead of constantly reassuring everybody that Obamacare was going to make things better, Obama should have been in Health and Human Services [HHS] Secretary Kathleen Sebelius' business like the drill sergeant from "An Officer and a Gentleman," insisting the HealthCare.gov website be ready for the Oct. 1 [2013] rollout.

Now the president looks like Professor Harold Hill, the flim-flam artist from "The Music Man" who promised River City a boys band with no intention of ever delivering. That may seem overly harsh—no one suggests Obama wanted his marquis domestic program to stumble.

Oversight Lacking

Yet where was the oversight? Heck, it has been reported that HealthCare.gov wasn't even fully tested until two weeks prior to go-time and that 24 hours after it opened for business, only six people had managed to sign up.

A good leader knows when to get personally involved and when to leave something to his subordinates.

That said, the website failures are not the end of the world. It's a website, not a nuclear weapons verification treaty. Health Care.gov can be fixed. But it needs to be fixed soon or fast workarounds found to make sure that everyone who wants to sign up or wants to explore his or her options for switching insurance can do so in a secure, efficient and reliable way.

After successfully staring down the more radical wing of the congressional Republicans who shut down the government in an attempt to defund Obamacare, the president could have scored even more points by delivering what he's been promising for more than three years.

Instead, Obama's popularity has dropped through the floor. You can bet the Republican Party is salivating at the opportunity for big gains during next year's midterm elections.

Damage Control

So, what now? Sebelius testified before Congress that she's accountable for the mess while Obama has said the problems need to get fixed, ASAP. Ya think.

The rollout of Obamacare was always about the details, and yet Obama has come across as disconnected from the whole process.

It's almost unimaginable that Obama could be so careless as to have allowed his signature legislation to debut so miserably.

He needs to re-engage quickly. He must keep Sebelius in office only because it would be more disruptive to the process to fire her—but he needs to be omnipresent at HHS until this is fixed. If the U.S. government can sweep up the phone calls of millions of Americans and most of the leaders in Europe, surely it can figure out how to get one website operating.

Obama has also been rapped, rightly, for his misstatement that everyone who wanted to could keep his or her health insurance plans could do so. Obviously that was a gross exaggeration. A number of Americans with individual plans are getting cancellation notices.

All Roads Lead to HealthCare.gov

Yes, as the president suggests, most of these plans were probably lousy to begin with and now don't meet the standards of Obamacare. But when Obama then says that all that people have to do is shop around for a better deal, we're back to the problem website. The very portal that allows all of this to take place isn't up to snuff.

It's almost unimaginable that Obama could be so careless as to have allowed his signature legislation to debut so miserably. He has let down millions of uninsured Americans and lost the faith of perhaps millions more who thought he was on the right track.

In one sense, he is on the right track. Making sure that all Americans have access to decent health care and preventative care while also trying to slow the pace of medical cost inflation remain essential to the U.S. economy.

That's why Obama needs to recommit himself to bringing his health care reforms to fruition before they derail entirely.

15

Despite a Botched Rollout, the Health-Care Law Is Worth It

Alan S. Blinder

Alan S. Blinder is a professor of economics and public affairs at Princeton University and former vice chairman of the Federal Reserve. He is the author of After the Music Stopped: The Financial Crisis, the Response, and the Work Ahead.

The website troubles that christened the arrival of the Affordable Care Act (ACA) made a big impression on the American public, and it wasn't a favorable one. Unfortunately, one poorly designed website overshadowed all of the positive things about the law. Critics seized on these glitches and other enrollment difficulties as evidence that the ACA is doomed to fail, and the public relations (PR) spin has been very successful in that regard. President Barack Obama added to the PR nightmare with his infamous remark, made before the rollout of the website, that if you like your health plan and doctors you could keep them, when in reality many plans were cancelled by insurers after the ACA enrollment period began. That said, nothing ever goes as planned and the negative spin about the ACA is exactly that: spin. It is clear that the ACA's troubles are much more about bad PR than bad policy.

The botched rollout of the Patient Protection and Affordable Care Act (commonly called the ACA or "ObamaCare") has been an unmitigated disaster. Choose your favorite adjective: horrible, embarrassing, inexcusable. They all fit.

But a badly designed website doesn't signify a badly designed policy. The goals, principles and major design features of the ACA are barely affected by the government's health-exchange website catastrophe. If you liked the basic ideas before, you still should. If you didn't, you still shouldn't.

Unfortunately, that simple message may not penetrate the public consciousness. I fear that what is being sloughed off by some ACA supporters as merely bad PR might wind up being a great deal more damaging. Remember, in politics, spin is often more important than reality.

Many Republicans have been unremittingly hostile to the ACA since it passed Congress. They have never stopped trying to kill or obstruct it, and they have not been constrained by the truth. (Remember "death panels"?) The website debacle hands them a gift: a line of attack that is true and legitimate.

While Americans either read about or experience the website's failures firsthand, the enemies of health-care reform are telling them that ObamaCare is a failure. And since virtually no one actually understands how the new law works, the verdict sounds plausible. Thus tech "glitches" make the law's critics look better and make the administration look like the gang that couldn't shoot straight.

You only get one chance to make a first impression, and many Americans' first impression of health-care reform comes from the website—or from jokes about it by [comedians Jay] Leno, [David] Letterman and [Jon] Stewart. Becoming a national laughingstock is worse than getting off to a bad start. It undermines trust in health-care reform and, more generally, in the government's ability to solve problems.

And it's not just website problems. Americans are also hearing more and more about a second snafu. (Remember what those five letters stand for.) The president assured people over and over again that "if you like your [health insurance] plan, you can keep it." Well, it turns out that maybe you can't; your current insurance might get canceled.

Supporters of ObamaCare point out that such cases are a small minority, and they occur only with subpar plans. True. But that "small minority" is millions of cases, and that carries weight. Indeed, movements are already afoot in Congress—involving both Republicans and Democrats—to change the law to make President Obama's pledge true.

There is at least some reason to think that the "affordable care" part of the [ACA] may be working already. The rate of inflation of medical costs has tumbled in recent years.

If we could get people to turn their attention from PR to policy—a big if—they would see that little has changed. The three central elements of ObamaCare are insurance reform, getting (most of) the uninsured covered, and containing the upward spiral in medical-care costs. Each remains in place.

Regarding coverage, while the health-exchange website's problems are causing delays, they will be fixed—though I'm not sure I'd bet on Nov. 30. (If the administration makes that deadline, someone deserves a medal.) The initial enrollment period might have to be extended a bit, which would require some other adjustments. But even with delays, most of the uninsured will be able to get covered.

Nor are the central elements of insurance reform affected by the technology glitches. Millions of people under the age of 26 are already benefiting by being kept on their parents' policies. Pre-existing conditions will no longer prevent people from getting health insurance. Annual and lifetime limits will go the way of the dodo. Americans will like all that.

Regarding cost containment, some of the law's planned demonstration and pilot programs, designed to test various cost-reducing ideas, might be delayed. But they won't be abandoned. Delays will hurt a bit because these experiments were destined to take years to complete in any case, and our political system is not known for patience. But there is at least some reason to think that the "affordable care" part of the act may be working already. The rate of inflation of medical costs has tumbled in recent years.

All that said, no big social policy ever goes exactly as planned. Two additional hazards that have garnered relatively little attention to date worry me.

The first is the behavior of the "invincibles"—young people who, statistically speaking, are at little risk for high medical bills. To make universal coverage work, the government needs to bring them into the insurance pool as counterweights to the high-risk people. But the "individual mandate" is not really a mandate. The law allows people to opt out by paying a modest fee: just 1% of income in the first year, which is a mere $500 for someone with a $50,000 income. That is a pittance compared with the cost of most health-insurance policies. If many low-risk people stay out of the pool, we have a problem: The insured pool will be less healthy than the total population.

Second, there's the behavior of businesses with more than 50 employees. Some companies that now cover their workers with costly health-care plans might decide to drop that coverage once the exchanges are up and running. The penalty for leaving workers uncovered is just $2,000 per person per year, and the exchanges will make insurance available to all. So pure self-interest will push firms to drop coverage. Will we rely on altruism, peer group pressure and employee demands to push back?

Considering all these problems, is the game worth the candle? Absolutely—because the status quo ante was so unacceptable. America cannot be a humane society if we leave 15% of our population uninsured. America cannot be an efficient society if we spend 50% to 100% more of our incomes on health care than other countries, and yet don't get better health outcomes. We can't let a botched website get in the way of goals that big.

Organizations to Contact

The editors have compiled the following list of organizations concerned with the issues debated in this book. The descriptions are derived from materials provided by the organizations. All have publications or information available for interested readers. The list was compiled on the date of publication of the present volume; the information provided may change. Be aware that many organizations take several weeks or longer to respond to inquiries, so allow as much time as possible.

American Medical Association (AMA)
AMA Plaza, 330 N. Wabash Ave., Suite 39300
Chicago, IL   60611-5885
(800) 621-8335
website: www.ama-assn.org

Founded in 1847, the American Medical Association (AMA) is the primary professional association of physicians in the United States. It disseminates information concerning medical breakthroughs, medical and health legislation, educational standards for physicians, and other issues concerning medicine and health care. The AMA supports the Affordable Care Act and lobbied for it in Congress and is now working with legislators to refine its provisions. AMA activities in this area are summarized in the article "Advocating for Improvements to the Affordable Care Act," and documents related to its efforts are also available on the organization's website. The AMA operates a library and offers many publications, including the weekly journal, *JAMA*; the weekly newspaper, *American Medical News*; and journals covering specific types of medical specialties.

Cato Institute
1000 Massachusetts Ave. NW, Washington, DC   20001-5403
(202) 842-0200 • fax: (202) 842-3490
website: www.cato.org

The Cato Institute is a libertarian public policy research foundation dedicated to limiting the role of government, protecting individual liberties, and promoting free markets. As such, Cato has opposed the Affordable Care Act (ACA) since its inception and is working to effect its reversal. The institute's website features a variety of publications related to the ACA, including books, monographs, multimedia and video presentations, briefing papers, and other studies. Recent titles include "The Libertarian State of the Union: The Future of the Affordable Care Act," "Four Ways to Actually Defund the Affordable Care Act," and "A Conspiracy Against Obamacare." Among Cato's regular publications are the quarterly magazine *Regulation*, the bimonthly *Cato Policy Report*, and the periodic *Cato Journal*.

HealthCare.gov
Centers for Medicare & Medicaid Services
7500 Security Blvd., Baltimore, MD 21244
(800) 318-2596
website: www.healthcare.gov

HealthCare.gov is the federal government's online insurance marketplace for consumers to obtain health coverage through the Affordable Care Act (ACA). The site offers extensive information about the ACA, including details about eligibility for individuals, families, and small businesses; how to calculate coverage costs and sign up for insurance through the marketplace; descriptions of covered services and how to access care; and implementation, policy, and regulatory information. The site features a frequently updated blog as well as a collection of videos that feature people talking about why having health care is important to them. The media section of the site links to the US Department of Health and Human Services website, which offers additional background information on the ACA.

The Heritage Foundation
214 Massachusetts Ave. NE, Washington, DC 20002-4999
(202) 546-4400
website: www.heritage.org

The Heritage Foundation is a conservative think tank that works to create and advocate for public policies that promote the ideals of free enterprise, limited government, individual freedom, traditional American values, and a strong national defense. The organization has strongly opposed the Affordable Care Act and its website includes hundreds of issue briefs, research papers, commentaries, blog posts, and infographics on the topic. Publications available online include "How the Affordable Care Act Is Killing Jobs," "The Affordable Care Act Isn't," and "Ten Broken Obamacare Promises."

National Economic and Social Rights Initiative (NESRI)
90 John St., Suite 308, New York, NY   10038
(212) 253-1710 • fax: (212) 385-6124
e-mail: info@nesri.org
website: www.nesri.org

The National Economic and Social Rights Initiative (NESRI) is a nonprofit that works with communities to build a broad movement for economic and social rights, including health, housing, education, and work with dignity. The organization supports the idea of universal health care as a human right and has been critical of the Affordable Care Act (ACA) because it believes the act does not go far enough toward meeting that ideal. NESRI authors frequently write feature articles and opinion pieces on the ACA that appear in publications worldwide, and the group's website features those published works as well as blog postings and links to news items related to the ACA and health care in general.

National Institutes of Health (NIH)
9000 Rockville Pike, Bethesda, MD   20892
(301) 496-4000
e-mail: NIHinfo@od.nih.gov
website: www.nih.gov

Founded in 1887, the National Institutes of Health (NIH) is one of the world's foremost medical research centers as well as the federal focal point for medical research in the United

States. The NIH, which comprises twenty-seven separate institutes and centers, is one of eight health agencies of the Public Health Service, which in turn is part of the Department of Health and Human Services. Resources available on the NIH website include dozens of reports related to the Affordable Care Act, including "Physicians, the Affordable Care Act, and Primary Care: Disruptive Change or Business as Usual?," "How the Affordable Care Act Will Strengthen the Nation's Primary Care Foundation," and "Impact of the New US Health-Care-Reform Legislation on the Pharmaceutical Industry: Who Are the Real Winners?"

Pew Research Center
1615 L St. NW, Suite 700, Washington, DC   20036
(202) 419-4300 • fax: (202) 419-4349
website: www.pewresearch.org

Pew Research Center is a nonpartisan research organization that informs the public about the issues, attitudes, and trends shaping America and the world. It conducts public opinion polling, demographic research, media content analysis, and other empirical social science research. Pew Research does not take policy positions. It is a subsidiary of the Pew Charitable Trusts, an independent nonprofit research organization. The Pew Research Center has extensively studied various aspects of the Affordable Care Act (ACA) and its website features more than 650 publications related to the ACA, including a wide variety of fact sheets, reports, and studies.

Urban Institute Health Policy Center (HPC)
2100 M St. NW, Washington, DC   20037
(202) 261-5640
e-mail: UIHealthPolicy@urban.org
website: www.urban.org/health_policy

The Urban Institute is a nonprofit, nonpartisan research organization that gathers data, conducts research, evaluates programs, offers technical assistance overseas, and educates Americans on social and economic issues with the goal of fostering sound public policy and effective government. The Health Policy Center (HPC) at the Urban Institute analyzes trends and underlying causes of changes in health insurance coverage, access to care, and use of health-care services by the entire US population. The HPC website features a broad collection of research related to the Affordable Care Act, including its ongoing "Health Reform Monitoring Survey" and the recent publications "Reaching and Enrolling the Uninsured: Early Efforts to Implement the Affordable Care Act" and "Medicaid and the Young Invincibles Under the Affordable Care Act: Who Knew?"

US Department of Health and Human Services (HHS)
200 Independence Ave. SW, Washington, DC   20201
(877) 696-6775
website: www.hhs.gov

The US Department of Health and Human Services is the federal government's principal agency for providing essential human services, especially for those who are least able to help themselves. Among its many public health responsibilities, HHS administers the Medicare, Medicaid, and Affordable Care Act (ACA) programs. The HHS website offers extensive information about the ACA, including information about eligibility, how to sign up through the health-care marketplace at HealthCare.gov, implementation details, covered services, state-by-state statistics, numerous fact sheets, and the complete text of the law.

US Senate
Washington, DC   20510
(202) 224-3121
website: www.senate.gov

The US Senate is the upper house of the bicameral legislature in Washington, DC. Along with the House of Representatives, it comprises the United States Congress. One of the Senate's functions is to create bills and get them approved as laws by both houses of Congress. The US Senate's website includes an extensive collection of documents related to the Affordable Care Act (ACA), ranging from transcripts of congressional testimony, statements about health-care reform by individual senators, news updates, press releases, and information about the many legislative efforts related to the Affordable Care Act's creation, implementation, and prospective future. Contact information for individual senators is also listed on the site.

The White House

1600 Pennsylvania Ave. NW, Washington, DC   20500
(202) 456-1111
website: www.whitehouse.gov

Nearly fifty-two thousand documents related to the Affordable Care Act (ACA) are available from the White House website, and a special section of the president's website is devoted to health-care reform. Resources available from the site include presidential statements and the text of speeches about the Affordable Care Act, in-depth fact sheets and information about the ACA, statistical reports, essays, news articles, press releases, blog posts, videos, interactive maps, and links to other useful resources, such as the health insurance marketplace at www.HealthCare.gov.

Bibliography

Books

Randy Barnett
et al.
A Conspiracy Against Obamacare: The Volokh Conspiracy and the Health Care Case. New York: Palgrave Macmillan, 2013.

Elizabeth Bradley,
Lauren Taylor,
and Harvey
Fineberg
The American Health Care Paradox: Why Spending More Is Getting Us Less. New York: Perseus, 2013.

Michael Cannon
and Michael
Tanner, eds.
Replacing Obamacare. Washington, DC: Cato Institute, 2013.

Stephen Davidson
A New Era in US Health Care: Critical Next Steps Under the Affordable Care Act. Palo Alto, CA: Stanford University Press, 2013.

William Dhiel
The ObamaCare Handbook: Understanding the Basics of the Patient Protection and Affordable Care Act of 2010. Fort Mill, SC: Quill, 2013.

Ezekiel Emanuel
Reinventing American Health Care. New York: PublicAffairs, 2014.

Guy Faguet
The Affordable Care Act: A Missed Opportunity, a Better Way Forward. New York: Algora, 2013.

Lawrence Jacobs and Theda Skocpol   *Health Care Reform and American Politics: What Everyone Needs to Know*. New York: Oxford University Press, 2013.

Barack Obama and the 111th US Congress   *The Patient Protection and Affordable Care Act*. Washington, DC: US Government Printing Office, 2012.

Chinyere Ogbonna   *A Different Perspective on the Patient Protection and Affordable Care Act.* Lanham, MD: University Press of America, 2013.

Wendell Potter   *Obamacare: What's in It for Me? What Everyone Needs to Know About the Affordable Care Act*. New York: Bloomsbury, 2013.

T.R. Reid   *The Healing of America: A Global Quest for Better, Cheaper, and Fairer Health Care*. New York: Penguin, 2010.

Harry Selker and June Wasser   *The Affordable Care Act as a National Experiment: Health Policy Innovations and Lessons*. New York: Springer, 2013.

Paul Starr   *Remedy and Reaction: The Peculiar American Struggle over Health Care Reform*. New Haven, CT: Yale University Press, 2013.

Michael D. Tanner   *Bad Medicine: A Guide to the Real Costs and Consequences of the New Health Care Law*. Washington, DC: Cato Institute, 2011.

Washington Post   *Landmark: The Inside Story of America's New Health-Care Law—The Affordable Care Act—and What It Means for Us All.* New York: PublicAffairs, 2010.

Periodicals and Internet Sources

AARP   "Health Law Fact Sheets," 2013. www.aarp.org.

Mark Adomanis   "Think Obamacare Is Socialized Medicine? 5 Things You Should Know About Soviet Healthcare," *Forbes*, September 25, 2013.

Jeffrey Anderson   "Bailing Out Health Insurers and Helping Obamacare," *Weekly Standard*, January 13, 2014. www.weeklystandard.com.

Jim Angle   "Almost 80 Million with Employer Health Care Plans Could Have Coverage Canceled, Experts Predict," Fox News, November 26, 2013. www.foxnews.com.

Peter Baker   "Democrats Embrace Once Pejorative 'Obamacare' Tag," *New York Times*, August 3, 2012.

James Beattie and Michael W. Chapman   "Ben Carson Warns: 'Socialized Medicine Is Keystone to Establishment of a Socialist State,'" CNSNews.com, October 11, 2013. http://cnsnews.com.

Melinda Beck — "Battles Erupt over Filling Doctors' Shoes," *Wall Street Journal*, February 5, 2013. http://online.wsj.com.

Jennifer Bergen et al. — "Funding Health Care as a Basic Human Right," *RNJournal*, December 2013.

Joe Biden — "Affordable Care Act: A Land of Options or Socialized Medicine?," *Atlanta Journal-Constitution*, October 2, 2013. http://blogs.ajc.com.

John Blake — "The Obamacare 'Scandal' You Haven't Heard About," CNN, November 8, 2013. http://religion.blogs.cnn.com.

Michael R. Blood — "Health Exchanges Slow to Attract Young, Healthy," Associated Press, November 15, 2013. http://bigstory.ap.org.

Patrick Brennan — "Sorry, Mr. President, There Is 'Serious Evidence' Obamacare Is Bad for Economic Growth," *National Review*, September 16, 2013.

Michael Cannon — "The Obstacle Is That Americans Don't Want It," *New York Times*, May 29, 2013.

David Catron — "Is Obamacare Socialism or Fascism?," *American Spectator*, January 18, 2013.

Centers for
Medicare and
Medicaid Services
"Covering People with Pre-Existing Conditions: Report on the Implementation and Operation of the Pre-Existing Condition Insurance Plan Program," January 31, 2013. www.cms.gov.

Niraj Chokshi
"Many States with Few Insured Citizens Aren't Expanding Medicaid Under Obamacare," *Washington Post*, September 17, 2013. www.washingtonpost.com/blogs.

Lisa Chow
"3 Ways Obamacare Is Changing How a Hospital Cares for Patients," National Public Radio, November 26, 2013. www.npr.org/blogs.

Council for
Affordable Health
Insurance
"Health Insurance Mandates in the States 2012: Executive Summary," April 9, 2013. www.cahi.org.

David M. Cutler
"The Economics of the Affordable Care Act," *New York Times*, August 7, 2013. http://economix.blogs.nytimes.com.

John Daniel
Davidson
"Obamacare as Civil Right," *First Things*, September 5, 2013. www.firstthings.com.

Carmen
DeNavas-Walt,
Bernadette D.
Proctor, and
Jessica C. Smith
"Income, Poverty, and Health Insurance Coverage in the United States: 2011," US Census Bureau, September 2012. www.census.gov.

Drew Desilver   "Most Uninsured Americans Live in States That Won't Run Their Own Obamacare Exchanges," Pew Research Center, September 19, 2013. www.pewresearch.org.

Mike Emanuel   "Second Wave of Health Plan Cancellations Looms," Fox News, November 20, 2013. www.foxnews.com.

Dylan Ewers   "How Obamacare Will Hurt Tax Payers and Stop the Economic Recovery," PolicyMic, April 26, 2012. www.policymic.com.

Linda Feldmann   "Obamacare: 'Job-Killer' or Freedom from 'Job Trap'?," *Christian Science Monitor*, February 6, 2014.

Garance Franke-Ruta   "The New Problem with Obamacare Isn't Socialism, It's Creative Destruction," *Atlantic*, October 29, 2013.

Gerald Friedman   "A Century and Counting: The Campaign for National Health Insurance," Democratic Socialists of America, September 30, 2013. www.dsausa.org.

Bruce Frohnen   "Obamacare Is Government Run Healthcare," *Crisis Magazine*, March 18, 2013.

Maggie Gallagher   "A Basic Human Right to Obamacare?," TownHall, August 25, 2010. http://townhall.com.

Scott Gottlieb — "Medicaid Is Worse Than No Coverage at All," *Wall Street Journal*, March 10, 2011.

Peter Grier — "'Obamacare' vs. 'Affordable Care Act': Does the Name Matter?," *Christian Science Monitor*, November 29, 2013.

Sanjay Gupta — "Better Health Not About Obamacare, It's About You," CNN, December 2, 2013. www.cnn.com.

Craig Harrington and Albert Kleine — "How Print and Broadcast Media Are Hiding Obamacare's Success In Controlling Costs," Media Matters for America, November 27, 2013. http://mediamatters.org.

Heritage Foundation — "Obamacare: Top 10 Reasons It's Wrong for America," July 30, 2009. www.heritage.org.

Joshua Holland — "The Biggest Problem with Obamacare's Rollout Is Being Caused Intentionally by Republicans," BillMoyers.com, November 21, 2013. http://billmoyers.com.

W.W. Houston — "Implementing Obamacare: The Rate-Shock Danger," *Economist*, June 4, 2013. www.economist.com/blogs.

Chris Jacobs — "Obamacare: Taking Away Americans' Health Coverage," *The Foundry*, August 6, 2013. http://blog.heritage.org.

Risa Kaufman   "A Human-Rights Lens on the
                        Affordable Care Act," *Huffington Post*,
                        March 28, 2012. www.huffingtonpost
                        .com.

Sarah Kliff   "Obamacare Needs Young People to
                        Sign Up. And It Looks Like They're
                        Starting," *Washington Post*, October
                        11, 2013.

Sarah Kliff   "We Still Don't Know the Most
                        Important Obamacare Enrollment
                        Number," *Washington Post*, November
                        14, 2013.

Paul R. La   "Obamacare's Big Winners: Insurers.
Monica   Oops!," CNNMoney, November 21,
                        2013. http://buzz.money.cnn.com.

Allison Linn   "You Think the Obamacare Fight Is
                        Ugly?," CNBC, October 1, 2013.
                        www.cnbc.com.

Annie Lowrey   "Study Finds Health Care Use Rises
                        with Expanded Medicaid," *New York
                        Times*, May 2, 2013.

Anna Wilde   "Many Health Insurers to Limit
Mathews   Choices of Doctors, Hospitals," *Wall
                        Street Journal*, August 15, 2013.

John Mauldin   "Obamacare Will Change
                        Everything—And I Think It Might
                        Cause a Recession," *Business Insider*,
                        October 6, 2013. www.businessinsider
                        .com.

Stephanie Mencimer   "The Latest Legal Attack Against Obamacare," *Mother Jones*, December 3, 2013.

Jason Millman   "Small Business Obamacare Online Enrollment Delayed a Year," *Politico*, November 28, 2013. www.politico .com.

Casey B. Mulligan   "Health Care Inflation and the Arithmetic of Labor Taxes," *New York Times*, August 7, 2013. http:// economix.blogs.nytimes.com.

Nisha Nathan   "Doctor Shortage Could Cause Health Care Crash," ABC News, November 13, 2012. http:// abcnews.go.com.

Jaisal Noor and Wendell Potter   "Disastrous Rollout of Obamacare Should Shift Focus to Universal Healthcare Part I," The Real News Network, December 2, 2013. http://therealnews.com.

Matthew Rousu   "Obamacare Won't Make Healthcare More Affordable: Here's What Will," *Forbes*, November 27, 2013.

Juilie Rovner   "The Healthy, Not the Young, May Determine Health Law's Fate," National Public Radio, January 24, 2014. www.npr.org/blogs.

San Francisco Bay Guardian   "Single-Payer Is the Cure," November 19, 2013.

Peter Schweizer   "At Least One Group of Americans Loves ObamaCare," Fox News, November 12, 2013. www.foxnews .com.

Billy Sellers   "Obamacare Inches Us Toward Socialism," *Alexander City Outlook*, November 11, 2013. www.alexcityoutlook.com.

Casey Selwyn   "'Obamacare' Isn't as Bad—or Good—as You've Heard," *Christian Science Monitor*, February 25, 2014.

Alyene Senger   "Obamacare's Impact on Today's and Tomorrow's Taxpayers—An Update," Heritage Foundation, Issue Brief No. 4022, August 21, 2013. www.heritage.org.

Alyene Senger   "Obamacare's Impact on Doctors—An Update," Heritage Foundation, Issue Brief No. 4024, August 23, 2013. www.heritage.org.

Mark Silva   "#Obamacare: Bad Word, Good Word," Bloomberg, September 26, 2013. http://go.bloomberg.com.

Shannon Vitiritti   "Obamacare Is Not Socialized Medicine," Examiner.com, August 25, 2012. www.examiner.com.

White House   "24 States Are Refusing to Expand Medicaid. Here's What That Means for Their Residents," November 6, 2013. www.whitehouse.gov.

Index